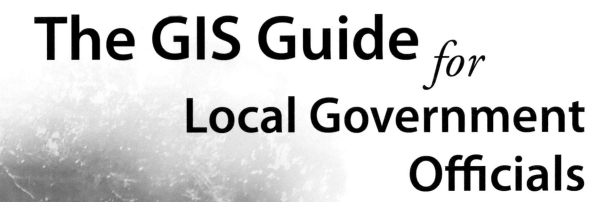

The GIS Guide *for* Local Government Officials

Edited by **Cory Fleming**,
International City/County
Management Association (ICMA)

ESRI PRESS
REDLANDS, CALIFORNIA

ESRI Press, 380 New York Street, Redlands, California 92373-8100

Copyright © 2005 ESRI

All rights reserved. First edition 2005
10 09 08 07 06 05   1 2 3 4 5 6 7 8 9 10

Printed in the United States of America

Library of Congress Cataloging-in-Publication Data
The GIS guide for local government officials / edited by Cory Fleming.—1st ed.
    p. cm.
  Includes index.
    ISBN 1-58948-141-0 (pbk. : alk. paper)
    1. Local governmen—Information technology—United States. 2. Local government—Technological innovations—
    United States. 3. Geographic information systems—United States. I. Fleming, Cory, 1963-
  JS344.E4.G57 2005
  352.3'8214'0285--dc22   2005020877

Ask for ESRI Press titles at your local bookstore or order by calling 1-800-447-9778. You can also shop online at www.esri.com/esripress. Outside the United States, contact your local ESRI distributor.

ESRI Press titles are distributed to the trade by the following:

In North America, South America, Asia, and Australia:
Independent Publishers Group (IPG)
Telephone (United States): 1-800-888-4741
Telephone (international): 312-337-0747
E-mail: frontdesk@ipgbook.com

In the United Kingdom, Europe, and the Middle East:
Transatlantic Publishers Group Ltd.
Telephone: 44 20 8849 8013
Fax: 44 20 8849 5556
E-mail: transatlantic.publishers@regusnet.com

Cover design by Savitri Brant
Book design and production by Savitri Brant
Copyediting by Tiffany Wilkerson
Print production by Cliff Crabbe
Cover photograph by Milton Ospina

In memory of William J. McGill, a dedicated public servant and national leader
in local government management

Contents

Foreword

Local government operates in a complex, constantly changing environment. Managing local government today challenges leaders to think beyond our traditional approaches to innovation and everyday problem solving. For nearly a century, the International City/County Management Association (ICMA) has promoted excellence in local government management by providing information and tools local leaders need to respond to the challenges of this constantly changing environment.

As a part of this tradition, ICMA is pleased to have worked with ESRI on this volume to help local government leaders better understand how geographic information systems (GIS) technology can benefit their organization. We recruited authors who understand the complexities of local government and have hands-on experience in introducing and implementing a GIS in local government. They know what it takes to make a GIS a success, and they have generously shared their talents and knowledge in this volume.

GIS offers local government leaders a valuable tool for assessing and dealing with change. GIS provides a way to gather data from very diverse sources and look at it in a systematic fashion. It greatly reduces the amount of time needed to analyze problems within a community—whether the problem is crime statistics by neighborhood, alternative building scenarios for development, or assessing the property tax structure—and allows leaders to quickly determine appropriate responses. GIS has revolutionized the way communities and local government leaders approach daily operations and management, giving them the ability to improve both efficiency and effectiveness in delivering services to their citizens.

I encourage you to use this book as a thinking tool and begin to imagine what benefits a GIS could bring to your community.

Robert J. O'Neill, Jr.
Executive Director
International City/County Management Association

Acknowledgments

This volume is the result of a rather extraordinary collaboration involving many dedicated and talented individuals. A debt of gratitude is owed to all of them for their unwavering perseverance and sense of humor in seeing this project through to its end.

First and foremost, the authors of this book—Eric Anderson, Patrick Bresnahan, Linda Gerull, Bill McGill, Don Oliver, and Barry Waite—volunteered to give up their weekends and evenings to research and write their chapters. These individuals went above and beyond the call of duty to help others in the field better understand the growing importance of GIS for local government. They are all teachers at heart and deserve a hearty round of applause for their efforts.

Sadly, one of our authors, Bill McGill, passed away on March 31, 2005, before this volume was published. His keen sense of humor and enthusiastic nature made planning sessions for the book truly enjoyable. His knowledge of both local government management and GIS technology helped focus discussions and added much to the overall content of this volume.

Numerous other individuals—their names can be found in the case studies throughout this book—freely gave their time to tell the story about how their local government GIS works. Their generous assistance with this volume was wonderful.

Chris Thomas, Milton Ospina, and Shelley Christensen at ESRI have provided valuable guidance and oversight throughout the development and production of the book. In addition to giving advice and feedback on the content, they helped research communities to feature in the case studies and identified important resources for local governments exploring the implementation of a GIS. Their expertise greatly enhanced the overall quality and value of the volume.

Within ICMA, Mosi Kitwana, Danielle Miller Wagner, David Borak, and Ryan Brueske served as content reviewers, offering suggestions on the organization and structure of the book. They also provided important moral support throughout the book's production.

Finally, many thanks go to Judy Hawkins, Mike Kataoka, and Savitri Brant with ESRI Press for their assistance in the final stages of the book's production. Their dedication to quality is most appreciated.

Cory Fleming
Editor
International City/County Management Association

Biographies

Cory Fleming
Editor
International City/County Management Association

As a senior project manager, Ms. Fleming conducts research on a variety of local government management issues. She has an extensive background in community and economic development, having worked with local governments, community groups, and nonprofit organizations on a variety of development issues for nearly a decade in the Midwest. Her interest in GIS began while working with scientists in Africa on the impact of land-use and land-cover change. GIS technology aided the scientists greatly in conveying the policy implications of their work to decision makers, and Ms. Fleming has been a believer ever since. She has a bachelor's degree from Iowa State University and a master's degree from the Johns Hopkins University.

Eric A. Anderson
City Manager
City of Tacoma, Washington

Mr. Anderson has more than thirty years of experience in local government management. He has been city manager for the City of Tacoma, Washington, since July 2005, and formerly was city manager for the City of Des Moines, Iowa. He has been actively involved in ICMA since the 1970s, including serving as the chair of ICMA's GIS Consortium. He has served on the National Research Council's Mapping Sciences Committee since 2000 and participated as a panel member in the development of the National Academy of Public Administration's report, *Geographic Information for the 21st Century: Building a Strategy for the Nation* in 1998. Mr. Anderson has written much about local government and its role in building the National Spatial Data Infrastructure (NSDI), an effort of the Federal Geographic Data Committee. He received his bachelor's degree from Syracuse University and master's degrees from the State University of New York at Albany and Syracuse University.

Patrick Bresnahan, PhD
Geographic Information Officer (GIO)
Richland County, South Carolina

Dr. Bresnahan has extensive experience in GIS technology. He participated in the Postgraduate Research Program offered by the U.S. Department of Energy (US DOE) and was awarded a Post-doctoral Research Fellowship sponsored by the Oak Ridge Institute for Science and Education. His post-doctoral research was conducted at the US DOE facility at the Savannah River Site. He has also received fellowship awards from AM/FM International (now GITA) and National Air and Space Administration (NASA) under the South Carolina Space Grant Consortium. Dr. Bresnahan maintains numerous professional memberships; his professional activities have included certification as a mapping scientist in GIS/LIS through the American Society for Photogrammetry and Remote Sensing, co-chairing the technology subcommittee of the South Carolina

State Mapping Advisory Committee, and participation in numerous federal agency geospatial planning and evaluation efforts. In emphasizing the importance of local government GIS operations, Dr. Bresnahan actively supports efforts of the ICMA. He also serves as a member of the National Association of Counties GIS subcommittee, and is an advisory board member of the Carolina Urban and Regional Information Systems Association. He earned his bachelor's degree from the University of Maryland-Baltimore County, a master's degree from Indiana State University, and a PhD from the University of South Carolina.

Linda Gerull
GIS Manager
Pierce County, Washington

Ms. Gerull joined Pierce County in 1994 as the GIS manager. She is responsible for managing the county's enterprise GIS, which includes software planning, design, development, and implementation as well as database construction. Ms. Gerull's leadership has resulted in more than $15 million of data construction. Pierce County's GIS currently supports seven hundred regional GIS customers in twenty-five county departments and ten subscribing agencies. The GIS has developed and supports more than sixty desktop and Web-based GIS business applications. Ms. Gerull has twenty years of GIS consulting and management experience. She has managed all phases of GIS system development and database construction for GIS projects in utility agencies, local government, departments of transportation, federal government (nationally and internationally), and commercial businesses. Her work experience includes senior positions with Intergraph Corporation and UGC Consulting. Ms. Gerull has a bachelor's degree from the University of Tennessee.

William J. McGill
ICMA Credentialed Manager

Mr. McGill worked in local government for more than three decades. He became a member of the International City/County Management Association in 1974 and earned the distinction of being an ICMA credentialed manager in 2004. His local government tenure includes serving as the village manager of Richton Park, Illinois, from 1977 to 1978; city manager of North Miami Beach, Florida, from 1984 to 1986; deputy city manager of Upper Arlington, Ohio, from 1987 to 1995; assistant city administrator of Billings, Montana, from 1995 to 2001; and information services director of Issaquah, Washington, from 2001 to 2004. He received his bachelor's degree from Pennsylvania State University and his master's degree from the Illinois Institute of Technology.

Donald R. Oliver
Fire Chief
Wilson, North Carolina

Chief Oliver is a thirty-eight-year veteran working in fire protection services. He began his career as a firefighter with the Wichita Kansas Fire Department in March 1967. As a member of the Thornton, Colorado, Fire Department from 1973 to 1992, his ranks included lieutenant, training officer, assistant chief, and chief of the department. He has served as the chief of the Wilson Fire/Rescue Service since March 1992. Chief Oliver received his bachelor's degree from Columbia College in Missouri. He also is a graduate of the National Fire Academy's Executive Fire Officer Program and the Management Excellence Program at the Center for Public Service with the University of Virginia.

Barry Waite
Geographic Information Systems Administrator
Carson, California

Mr. Waite has worked for the city of Carson, California, more than sixteen years, including four years in the city manager's office and four years as a city planner. In fact, he has worked for every department in the city except recreation. Mr. Waite has a master's degree from the University of Southern California and a GIS certificate from California State University, Long Beach. He is a planning commissioner for the city of Lomita, California, and serves on the board of directors for a nonprofit development company working in downtown Los Angeles.

Overview

Eric A. Anderson[1]
City Manager, City of Tacoma, Washington

As far back as the Stone Age, our distant ancestors likely sat around fires to consider, discuss, and probably argue about where they would find the best hunting. This was an important question—a question tied in part to geography—which determined not only the quality of their lives but also the likelihood of their survival. These ancient people, though, had limited information to help them make decisions. Certainly, they had primitive tools to process information. At best, they might have a drawing in the dirt indicating where the best hunting grounds were located.

Since that time, people have continued the struggle to make good decisions. The questions have changed over time, and most are no longer questions of survival. But many are still questions of geography, such as where to construct buildings, locate roads and railroads, or deliver private or governmental services. Information was, and still is, the key. As society became more sophisticated, information became a commodity. This is the Information Age with a highly complex economy based primarily on the conceptual quality and utility of information itself. Fortunately, the tools to process information have evolved greatly since those first early maps to the good hunting grounds.

Geographic information systems (GIS) give people the tools to thrive in the Information Age. A GIS provides ready access to a wide array of geographic information in an easy-to-understand format—a map. With this information, policy makers, planners, and the public alike can consider, discuss, and probably argue about a number of different issues—perhaps even where the best hunting grounds are—but they do so with a common understanding of the situation and the probable implications of their decisions.

According to William Huxhold, an urban planning professor and author, "good decisions require good information" (Huxhold 1991). If information is a commodity, then it must be managed as such. Producing good information requires tools—powerful tools to help people organize and think about data and information in new ways. Many of the current data collection systems in local governments are a by-product of an operations management approach. Information is collected in the course of doing business, but little thought is given to how the information might be used to help make better decisions. An information management approach takes a more global overview of the data collected by local government. It seeks to integrate the data to create a more comprehensive view of how local government programs and services can work more effectively. In short, an information management approach looks to produce good information for better decisions.

A GIS takes an information management approach to data. It provides the means to incorporate, visualize, and understand the relationships (or lack thereof) between different types of data to create new information. It allows decision makers to assess interrelationships from this information. A GIS also allows decision makers to present this information more clearly to the citizenry. While this book is focused on the benefits of GIS for local government, this new approach also greatly affects state and federal government.

For local government decision makers and managers, the advent and availability of GIS as a tool for better decision making has profound implications in three major areas:

- service delivery
- governance and public policy
- public information and community engagement

Service delivery

Local governments provide the essential services that affect the quality of life for citizens. They rely on local government for clean water, sanitary sewers, and sewage treatment; road construction and maintenance; and police, fire, and emergency medical response. While not immediately apparent to the casual observer, the local government delivery systems for these services are not autonomous; they are intimately interconnected. Police, fire, and public works are all provided in an interwoven fabric that only becomes obvious during major emergencies, such as the attacks on the World Trade Center and the Pentagon, or more common disasters such as floods, tornados, or hurricanes.

When GIS is understood and deployed effectively, it readily shows these interconnections among local government services. In more concrete terms, this enables the police department to work with the parks and recreation department to determine where additional recreational programs might curb juvenile vandalism and other crimes. The water and sewer department can assist the fire department by improving water pressure to fight a major fire. Or the transportation department can coordinate with the public works department on road maintenance efforts so city streets are not continually torn up and money is not wasted on repair work.

Service delivery systems are also intimately connected with the citizens they serve and offer a rich source of data. For example, the information gathered in police departments comes mostly from citizens. The numbers of calls to police, fire, public works, parks and recreation departments—and their content—provide tremendous amounts of information about what people need, want, do not want, and, by implication, do not care about. The locations of complaints and service delivery points can reveal emerging trends about what happens in the city and where. This type of data says a lot about what cities do, how they do it, and what they will need to do in the future.

Beyond these internal functions, GIS data can also be linked with state and federal mandates and service systems. State health departments regulate local practices and reporting. Local government planning follows the framework of the Federal Emergency Management Agency (FEMA) floodplain maps. Interstate highways structure the road systems of every city. The U.S. Environmental Protection Agency (EPA) promulgates requirements that affect local economic development efforts, particularly in older cities. The Occupational Safety and Health Administration (OSHA) governs safety practices in all service systems. These state and federal programs require local government information systems to support local decisions, document their effectiveness, and track the services rendered.

Information is simultaneously the fuel and the by-product of service delivery. Good information is absolutely necessary to assure that local government service delivery systems continue to be both efficient and effective. Understanding how that information works can be the foundation for the golden resource that will improve these very services, namely GIS-linked service delivery information systems.

Governance and public policy

Local government is also about governance, the self-governance of people in a given area. More than ever, successful public policy depends on the quality of information and information technology. Public policy is about values, but it is also about knowing what is going on and how people are affected by policies. This requires powerful information, delivered to decision makers in a transparent, understandable form that results in the best policy possible. Much of this information is buried in the very records created every day in the normal course of business.

Consider first how the public policy process works. Figure 1.1, based on work done at North Carolina State University (Danielson and White 1998), depicts a very integrated process that is highly dependent on information at each stage.

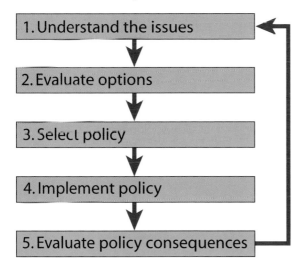

Figure 1.1   At every step in the local government policy process, information is produced and analyzed. A GIS can help produce the information for each step in a clear format.

Source: Based on drawing in *Using GIS in public policy analysis* (1998) by Leon Danielson and Nancy White, Design Research Laboratory, North Carolina State University, Raleigh, N.C. Reproduced by permission of Leon Danielson and Nancy White.

This cycle moves from steps one through five, repeating itself as issues are addressed and transformed. At each stage, there is an evaluation and feedback component based on the new information developed during the process. This feedback loop expresses the underlying fact that policy solutions create new policy challenges. A GIS can be extraordinarily useful in helping people understand all the implications of public policy issues and providing information throughout the process.

The first step in the policy cycle involves trying to grasp the essentials of an issue. When information is only anecdotal or displayed only in the charts and graphs, it is difficult to understand the problem in its full context. For example, suppose a city wants to determine if it has a problem with slumlords and where that problem might exist. A person could look for days at reams of charts and graphs that present data about housing violations, rental certificates, changes in property values, mortgage property sales, contract property sales, crime statistics, and abandoned vehicles and still not get as accurate an understanding as from looking at a map or maps that correlate all this information comprehensively and effectively.

Geographer Thomas Wilbanks points out that "public policy. . . is exquisitely geographic. . . spatial patterns, relationships and structures are at the heart of policy making" (Wilbanks 1985). At the local government level, public policy has always been about geography, specifically the relationship between people and places. An important function of GIS within the development of public policy, then, is to establish a system of collecting, organizing, and presenting information in a way that is easily understood. Imagine the difficulty of describing the boundary of a floodplain using only narrative. Then consider how easy this task becomes when using a map to actually show the area. GIS enables information to be visualized through mapping. It lets decision makers see information in an intuitively obvious format, namely a map. Seeing is believing.

Public information and community engagement

The last key area for GIS in local government is public information and community engagement. Local governments have an important responsibility to inform the public on a variety of issues; it is a matter of public trust that they do so. The challenge is providing that information and engaging the community in a manner that is meaningful and clear to all—not a small challenge given the complexity of issues with which most local governments must contend.

Providing services at the highest possible level and adequately supporting a successful policy process require not simply more information but information that can be used more effectively. For the most part, the current situation in many local governments can be characterized as follows:

- There is a great deal of unorganized raw data.
- This unorganized data is too valuable to ignore, but impossible to use effectively.
- Where systems do exist to organize information in meaningful ways, too often they are not integrated with other data systems; that is, the data systems are not interoperable.

The way local governments organize and use the data they collect needs to change. Primarily, local governments need to make better use of what they already have. To do this, the data must be

- organized in a well thought out way, and provisions should be made for its use
- contained in systems that are interoperable
- processed in ways that preserve its meaning and its coherence
- presented in easily understood ways that accurately and truthfully reflect its meaning
- documented fully and in a transparent manner

A GIS provides a platform to accomplish this through a single point of linkage, the geographic point of reference for the data.

GIS in local government

A GIS delivers solutions for local government in all three areas: service delivery, public policy and governance, and public information and community engagement. In each of these areas, local governments generate enormous amounts of data, and most has some element of geography associated with it. A GIS takes that data and uses the geographic element or physical location as its basis for organizing information. One tremendous benefit of a GIS is that once the information is organized for mapping, it can also be processed in other meaningful ways that make it more valuable and more helpful.

Joseph K. Berry, a GIS consultant and author, describes GIS as "a mapping tool, a spatial database management technology and an analytic revolution. But what may be its most important attribute is its ability to communicate. . . it fosters discussion that often leads to understanding and, ultimately, to effective decisions" (Berry 1993). The most important characteristic of a GIS is that it integrates information, making it far easier to communicate the impact of decisions in an understandable form.

Why is this communication element so important? Consider the value of being able to instantaneously see the impact of local government decisions, especially during an emergency. In the mid-1970s, a freight train wreck in the middle of a small New England town at 4:30 AM created a potentially disastrous situation. The train had derailed in a residential area with rolling hills and a river running through it. The train was hauling chemicals, consumer goods (including beer, which contains concentrated amounts of carbon dioxide), and a variety of other products, much of it unidentifiable to local responders. The beer spill released concentrated carbon dioxide. Other chemical cars remained intact, but there was uncertainty about their content and condition. Fire or explosion was a continual threat.

Police, firefighters, ambulance crews, public works personnel, neighbors, and a curious public all responded immediately. Railroad company employees also took action. Everyone worked hard to secure the train and its environs, to get the injured medical attention, and to reduce the potential hazards confronting the responders, those looking on, and the environment itself.

All of this happened without access to elevation maps to help identify low-lying areas where residents and other people were in danger of suffocation, since carbon dioxide sinks to the lowest point, displacing oxygen. They lacked adequate maps of the residential areas. They had no access to addresses and telephone numbers that would have enabled them to identify and advise neighborhood residents of the need to evacuate. The only means to notify residents was to visit each home, which represented a safety threat to personnel, given that the area had filled with carbon dioxide. They were unable to map plumes of released chemicals. Finally, they could not track their own vehicles and personnel to know who had gone where.

They did a masterful job, working together, using what limited information they had on hand. Almost all the information they needed was back at the office or in storage. But they couldn't get to it, integrate it, and use it well.

Today, an emergency situation without any recourse to available information should be as distant to local governments as that of man's ancestors sitting around a fire discussing where the best hunting grounds are. Local governments need not make life-saving decisions in a vacuum. GIS provides the means to gather information, analyze it, present it, and use it in real time.

Beyond emergency response, GIS offers many day-to-day advantages by providing strategically important information. Linking information to its location enables local government managers to understand the larger characteristics of their communities, such as zoning and land use, as well as the smaller details, such as the exact location of a manhole or fire hydrant. It helps track what has happened in the past to guide future service. For example, keeping domestic dispute histories readily available by address can inform police officers about what they are likely to encounter when called to a particular household. GIS also presents new ways to develop performance measures by linking inputs with outputs and outputs with outcomes.

GIS is a way to understand and use the information generated in one service system when working in another. For example, the information generated by the U.S. Army Corps of Engineers and FEMA concerning floodplains and floodways is critical in local zoning and building permitting. A map with flood information overlaid with a map of the parcels affected illuminates the risks associated with certain kinds of zoning and building. Furthermore, this information can be combined with telephone numbers—generated by corresponding addresses—to promptly notify imperiled residents of immediate threats to their lives and property.

GIS also charts underlying trends in physical areas of the city. With good data, local government can map a variety of features associated with the health of an area. For example, by simultaneously mapping a neighborhood's age of infrastructure, age of housing, mortgage sales, contract sales, police calls, crimes, health violations, housing violations, and other characteristics, it is possible to establish some measure of the health or quality of life for the residents of the neighborhood. This provides an effective and entirely new way to evaluate services provided to the neighborhood.

Finally, GIS is an effective tool for bridging the communication gap between governments and citizens by creating two-way conversations. In Des Moines, Iowa, interoperable systems enable citizens provided with handheld devices to enter requests for services directly into the city's work order system and then to track the response of the departments involved. GIS can also be used to aggregate information into clear map presentations that describe the important characteristics of the neighborhoods, as determined by the neighbors themselves. It enables them to direct the local service delivery system and then make their own judgment about the success of services as provided. To further engage citizens in the policy process, GIS can be used to help define the issues at stake in a policy decision or clarify the potential impact of a development proposal.

This book has been written by local government managers for local government managers. It is by no means a technical manual. Rather, it has been designed to help local government managers ponder how a GIS might help them better serve their communities. The focus is on providing concrete suggestions and examples of how a GIS can improve daily operations within local government. In chapter 2, William McGill dispels some long-standing myths of GIS and maps out the decision-making process for local government officials considering a GIS. Barry Waite takes an in-depth look at how to plan, implement, and fund a local government GIS in chapter 3. Donald Oliver discusses the possible internal uses for a GIS in chapter 4, while Linda Gerull looks at external services a local government GIS can offer in chapter 5. In chapter 6, Patrick Bresnahan provides a bird's-eye view of new trends and technologies emerging in the field. Finally, a list of useful resources for implementing a local government GIS is included at the back of this book.

This is a book about geographic information systems. More importantly, it is about how to manage local government better using GIS. This is not for just small cities and counties, or large ones. It is for all cities and counties. All services in local governments are provided to people at a specific location, typically their home and work addresses. Using these addresses as a means to develop, process, and present information is as important to the largest of local governments as it is to the smallest. In all cases, each citizen is the focus, the purpose, and the fundamental unit of local government. GIS is one of the most important ways to help serve these citizens well.

References

Berry, Joseph K. 1993. *Beyond mapping: Concepts, algorithms, and issues in GIS.* Fort Collins, Colo.: GIS World Books.

Danielson, Leon, and Nancy White. 1998 to present. Using GIS in public policy analysis: North Carolina. Raleigh, N.C.: Design Research Laboratory, North Carolina State University. Available online at www. ces.ncsu.edu/depts/design/research/WECO/policyGIS/index.html.

Huxhold, William. 1991. *An introduction to urban geographic information systems.* New York, N.Y.: Oxford University Press.

Wilbanks, Thomas J. 1985. Geography and public policy at the national scale. *Annals of the American Association of Geographers* vol. 75: 4–10.

Notes

1. Eric A. Anderson was city manager for the City of Des Moines, Iowa, when he wrote this chapter

2

Moving local government GIS from the tactical to the practical

William J. McGill[1]
Credentialed Manager, ICMA

Preface

The History Channel® series, *Tactical to Practical*, featured excellent examples of military and space technology being adapted for everyday, practical applications that enhance the quality of life. In much the same way, geographic information systems (GIS), once the province of highly complex engineering systems of geographic analysis, have become an integral part of local government technology applications. In fact, GIS integration is a standard feature and major selling point for practically all upgrades of basic local government data collection systems. For example, GIS components can be found in such diverse applications as finance, accounting, and billing; computer-aided dispatch for police and fire services; public works computer-aided design; and critical area mapping for inventories of infrastructure, natural resources, and property management.

What GIS has brought to all of these systems is on-demand data analysis of anything associated with a property or address. By overlaying different data types, one on top of another, local government managers and citizens can instantaneously see how different scenarios will play out in the community. As GIS has moved from its proprietary engineering and planning roots to the ubiquitous network desktop and even wireless applications, it has become indispensable as a strategic planning and decision-making tool.

From the perspective of local government and the local government manager, what is the value added by a GIS? Tactically, every local government has silos full of potential GIS data residing in each of its departments. From building permits to public safety incident reports, engineering project plans to planning preliminary plats, environmental impact to stream management and erosion studies—all of this information can be drawn upon by a GIS to see the effect of a decision. A GIS can stitch together data from the various departments, link the data to demonstrate corresponding relationships, and show those relationships on maps that are easy to understand.

For example, planning a new development in a mountainous and forested area with streams will have significant impact on soil content and erosion control. Among the factors that need to be considered are the potential for downstream flooding, habitat impact, and the number of units. All of these factors will influence impervious-surface water runoff and involve crucial engineering decisions for a storm water system and other infrastructure. In the past, such analysis required contracting for planning and engineering studies, using the very data already on hand in most local governments. With the advent of GIS, this data can be easily integrated into a single source for analysis. This value-added feature of a GIS allows local governments to transcend static maps and other professional studies into a more timely strategic analysis with "intelligent maps" that can illustrate various layers of data and their impact upon each area.

Rethinking GIS for small communities

In January 2002, the International City/County Management Association and ESRI sponsored a national webcast on using GIS for emergency preparedness and homeland security issues following the events of September 11. The discussion during the webcast emphasized the value of GIS as an analytical and decision-making tool for local government leaders, particularly with respect to emergency management. Participants clearly saw the benefits of GIS as a national asset, specifically for emergency management purposes, and more generally in all aspects of local government decision making. However, a number of questions arose concerning resources available to help small communities (less than 50,000 population) establish a GIS program. Most of the small local governments participating in the forum viewed GIS as a luxury beyond their reach.

Two years later, in 2004, the U.S. Department of Interior released findings from a survey undertaken as part of the Geospatial One-Stop System.[2] The survey gathered data about the use of GIS applications within local governments. Nearly twelve hundred local governments responded. Results indicate that GIS applications have become integral resources in local functions such as public works, public safety, and economic development. The survey found that about 97 percent of local governments with populations of more than 100,000 use GIS and about 88 percent of those between 50,000 and 100,000 use GIS. Among smaller governments, about 56 percent use GIS (Sarkar 2003). GIS applications among those surveyed breakdown as follows:

- viewing aerial photography: 77 percent
- supporting property record management and taxation services: 70 percent
- supplying public access information: 57 percent
- doing capital planning, design, and construction: 41 percent
- providing permitting services, emergency preparedness, and response: 38 percent
- offering computer-aided response: 33 percent
- supporting crime tracking and investigations: 28 percent

An overwhelming majority of survey respondents noted they would "allow the federal government to use their GIS data on floodplain mapping, land use, homeland security, and emergency preparedness and response" (Sarkar 2003). And repeating concerns voiced by participating smaller local governments during the 2002 webcast, the 2004 survey also identified two common barriers to GIS implementation: costs (64 percent) and lack of available technical expertise (42 percent).

In the two years from the webcast to the survey, local government officials became increasingly aware that GIS is more than just a national asset; it has direct benefits for small communities. GIS is no longer viewed as a luxury but a necessity for small communities. Further, survey participants identified a need to develop more regional projects, such as Geospatial One-Stop, for sharing information, data, and costs to develop a GIS infrastructure. "Homeland security funding could be an answer for such development. . . [with] an overwhelming majority of survey respondents [saying] building additional GIS layers and applications, maintaining data and providing training. . . could be improved with such homeland security funding to support those initiatives" (Sarkar 2003).

Despite this change in perspective, the basic problem for smaller local governments remains—how to overcome diminishing and competing funding and other resources as barriers to GIS development. But other less tangible and often more difficult barriers face GIS proponents in smaller local governments, namely a series of ingrained misconceptions or myths.

Persistent myths of GIS

Despite the fact that GIS is the focal point of practically every local government technology journal and countless new useful applications are coming online daily, five myths still persist that create roadblocks for developing GIS in small communities. Some are rooted in the historical development of GIS. Others stem from the propensity of many local governments to remain tied to organizational cultures that will not move beyond vertical management structures in governance and technological development.

Five GIS myths

1. GIS is too costly for smaller local governments, especially for communities with populations of 50,000 or less.
2. GIS is a proprietary application that requires specialized equipment, training, and integration with other municipal applications.
3. GIS is "compartmentalized" and useful only to engineering, planning, utilities, or other hard geographic and physical infrastructure analyses.
4. GIS does not lend itself to an immediate return on investment, since it requires an enormous time commitment to produce anything beyond "pretty, colored maps."
5. GIS is practical only for federal, state, and county governments, or large urbanized cities that have need of its massive data integration capabilities for macro analysis.

These myths are all related, but they need to be dispelled if the power of GIS analysis is to be harnessed for all sizes of local governments. These myths are examined in detail.

Myth #1: GIS is too costly for smaller local governments, especially for communities with populations of 50,000 or less.

As with most technology, GIS was once beyond the reach of all but the most advanced and resource-rich environments. The same could also be said of automobiles, telephones, and other personal communications devices, air travel, and computers. All these tools were once the province of only those who could afford and master them. But as they moved from the tactical to the practical, they proliferated in business and personal life. Consider, for example, Henry Ford's Model T®. When first introduced to the market in 1908, the car cost nearly $1,000—too expensive for the ordinary consumer at the time. By 1927, when the last Model T rolled off the production line, the car cost only about $300 and had changed daily life in America in a profound way.

GIS has followed a similar pattern. It has moved from tactically complex engineering and planning systems to computer desktop, laptop, and handheld devices. GIS started out with specialized applications, shifted to a Windows®-based, networked computing environment, and then went to Web-based GIS. It is now moving into wireless and handheld global positioning GIS applications, which can be purchased in retail stores. SimCity™, a series of computer games that imitates real-life scenarios, has been adapted to GIS. Almost anyone who can play a video game like SimCity can use GIS applications to create alternative scenarios to make decisions on a wide range of community issues. All of these developments have made GIS much easier to use and well within the budgets of most local governments.

With limited revenue, local governments have begun to realize that information technology, and particularly GIS, cannot be supported through a general fund revenue stream alone. As an enterprise technology, GIS benefits the governmental organization as a whole and should be supported in a like fashion. Pooling the resources of many different local government departments enables all to access a more robust GIS than if each individual department were to fund its own GIS. Software systems in many departments have incorporated GIS-based modules into their programs, collecting parcel and address data that can be captured and integrated as data layers for the GIS. Funding for these systems and the revenue streams they generate should be made available for GIS development.

The U.S. Department of Interior 2004 survey indicated that homeland security funding could be another answer. "GIS applications and solutions clearly resonate with emergency management and public safety executives as an essential tool to provide the most effective support of their efforts. . . .. An overwhelming majority of survey respondents said building additional GIS layers and applications, maintaining data and providing training. . . could be improved with such homeland security funding to support those initiatives" (Sarkar 2003).

Other options exist for funding GIS. If a local government is uncomfortable with the potential costs to implement a GIS on its own, it can combine resources with other local governments in the region. Coalitions of larger and smaller municipalities have formed across the country for this purpose. For example, the in-depth case study accompanying this chapter focuses on a group of thirteen municipalities in King County, Washington, that formed the eCityGov Alliance. By pooling resources, this coalition of communities developed several GIS applications to better serve their respective constituencies. Likewise, local governments, working together with other units of state and federal government, have further leveraged available resources by using common databases as a method to populate and integrate GIS for cross-jurisdictional applications.

A local government does not have to reinvent the wheel to take advantage of the many benefits offered by a GIS. Dramatically lower costs for technology, innovative funding strategies, and regional collaborative efforts make it possible for even the smallest of communities to tap into the power of a GIS.

Myth #2:   GIS is a proprietary application that requires specialized equipment, training, and integration with other municipal applications.

GIS used to require specialized software packages and high-end work stations that were limited in their use beyond highly technical purposes. And only those individuals who understood what buffers, nodes, rasters, and vectors were could make use of a GIS. It was a world of complex mystery that many techno-phobics feared.

But just as computer technology has evolved, so has GIS. GIS software applications are designed for desktop use, using drop-down menus and "point-and-click" technology commonly found in most PC and Macintosh® operating systems. Increased processing speed and expanded memory in modern personal computers has made specialized GIS work stations practically disappear.

A local government also can develop GIS applications without total dependency on proprietary GIS software applications. The growing need for user-oriented GIS applications has led to many new innovations in GIS technology. The Internet offers "new opportunities for distributing both geo-processing tools and geographic data to a wider range of potential users" (Zhao 2002). The requirements for a Web-based GIS are much different than other GIS, specifically with regard to expertise required, training needed, and intensity of user involvement. With Web-based GIS, the user does not work directly with a GIS software package, but instead uses an interface on an ordinary Web browser, such as Microsoft® Internet Explorer or Netscape® Navigator®, to access and work with the data. This essentially eliminates the need for additional software purchases, upgrades, and license fees for the casual GIS user. At the same time, it provides increased organizational access to mass quantities of data because any authorized user with an Internet connection can make use of the GIS.

GIS technology has become user-friendly and accessible for the general public. Many Web-based GIS applications—building permit systems, property locators, and others—are used routinely by residents who have no idea they are accessing a GIS database to find answers to their queries.

Myth #3:   GIS is "compartmentalized" and useful only to engineering, planning, utilities, or other hard geographic and physical infrastructure analyses.

As was the case with accounting, payroll, and utility billing systems, the roots of GIS technology can be traced in the United States to the U.S. Bureau of Census, which undertook an unprecedented program in computerized geography in the late 1960s. The explicit coding of the topology of street segments, with numbered nodes at each end and numbered areas on each side, was a major technological innovation that eventually revolutionized GIS (Mark et al. 1997). NASA and military satellite mapping programs also accelerated GIS by making greatly refined digital images of locations easily available.

For local governments, early compartmentalization of GIS resulted from partnerships with engineering consulting firms and municipal engineering departments to build federal and state survey grade data and address standards. In the early days of GIS, most local governments had neither the in-house technical expertise nor the financial resources to produce a stand-alone GIS on par with that maintained at the federal level. With the advent of Windows-based and desktop networked environments, followed by Web-based access and applications, and shared local and regional datasets during the last decade, GIS began to be recognized for its potential to affect every aspect of municipal data management.

But just as desktop computing applications such as spreadsheets and databases are no longer the exclusive jurisdiction of the finance department, GIS has crept beyond municipal land-use planning and CAD (computer-assisted design) engineering mapping programs. Marrying data to mapping made GIS the ultimate "governmental" information system since any data that can be tied to an address on a map makes it intelligent. Experts estimate that about 80 percent of data collected by governments has some kind of geographic component—such as a street address—and can be visualized using digital maps (Robinson 2002). Since most municipal services are tied to an address in a geographic location, every aspect of local government services can be tied to its geospatial physical, social, environmental, and economic impact.

By converting governmental data into data layers, a GIS can generate maps that illustrate themes much like the old plastic overlays in anatomy textbooks showed the various systems in the human body. Each data layer adds a new understanding of how the whole system functions. Ultimately, analyzing interrelated themes on one interactive map creates a mapping model that can be manipulated into decision-making scenarios limited only by the quantity and quality of the data. For example, combining census population data with the locations of existing child care facilities can help determine where additional facilities are needed. Such themes go well beyond the traditional uses of the planning and engineering departments. Local governments are using GIS analysis for such widely diverse needs as monitoring community health, tracking human services, locating community facilities such as parks and ball fields, and implementing pest control management.

The possibilities of how a GIS can improve all sorts of local government programs and services are endless. New, creative, and easy-to-use GIS applications are emerging constantly. "Information becomes more relevant when it's placed in a context that is meaningful to the individual, such as residents looking at crime displayed within their neighborhood boundaries, police officers viewing crimes or specific properties in their region of responsibility, or a company researching potential sites for relocation. Instead of someone else interpreting data, users perform their own query and analysis and draw their own conclusions" (Macgunigal 1999).

From a single-user system to an enterprise system in Oro Valley, Arizona

Oro Valley started out with only three town departments using GIS: public works, the police department, and the planning and zoning division within the community development department. A newly hired GIS team came on board in 2002 to move the system from a single-user based system to a multiuser enterprise system. But it faced tight budgets and skeptical management. To change this environment, the GIS team tackled four key issues:
- building support
- managing data
- enabling user access
- rethinking the organizational structure

Building support
The GIS team began by adopting a customer service–oriented approach where work for other departments was given top priority, ahead of GIS team priorities. The team also updated standardized maps and then automated the mapping process so new maps could easily be produced on a regular schedule. Revised procedures for handling special map requests enabled shorter turn-around times.

The team put new emphasis on training GIS users, developing new courses and offering training sessions at regular intervals. Finally, in an effort to rebuild communications with other departments, the GIS team interviewed directors and managers to learn more about their expectations for the GIS program. During the interviews, the team also laid out the goals it was trying to accomplish.

Managing data
Oro Valley's GIS data was spread out over multiple servers, and the level of quality varied considerably. The GIS team worked first to centralize the data and then improve data integrity and quality. The first step involved inventorying the current GIS data and locating it on a new central GIS server. After that, the team had to contend with multiple data formats created with different software programs. The GIS team researched available software products on the market and decided to move to a more manageable system known as geodatabase. With its increasing popularity and benefits, the team reasoned the software program could meet the town's growing needs for the foreseeable future. Once the software was in place, the team began converting its GIS data into the same format.

Enabling user access

As the GIS team continued to build the program, interest in the town's GIS grew. The team resolved to introduce nonusers to the new technology but had to contend with several issues—costs, training, and availability—in its effort to reach all town employees. Again, the GIS team researched possible software solutions to the issue. Ultimately it decided to move to an entirely Web-based GIS and worked with the town's information technology (IT) division on the development of an intranet site where all town employees could easily access the GIS. In doing so, the town was able to lower its overall software maintenance costs by 30 percent.

Rethinking organizational structure

When the GIS program began in Oro Valley, it was located in the planning and zoning division of the community development department. As the program grew, the work of the GIS team separated from the daily operations of the planning and zoning division. With the increased interest in GIS from other departments in the town, plans for a new organizational structure came into being. A merger with the IT division, which would enable a number of budgetary synergies, made sense. A newly revised GIS plan was developed to support the proposed structure and set standards for future GIS development.

Based on "Issues in building an enterprise GIS in small local government," by Raul Duato, a paper presented at the 2004 ESRI International User Conference, August 9–13, 2004 in San Diego, Calif.

Myth #4: GIS does not lend itself to an immediate return on investment, since it requires an enormous time commitment to produce anything beyond "pretty, colored maps."

In the past, local government officials resisted GIS because of the significant amount of initial investment necessary to get beyond producing static, one-dimensional, "pretty colored maps." Zoning maps, street maps, facilities maps, and the like generally have a specific and rather limited use. Up until the mid-1990s, this was indeed a valid argument by elected and appointed local government leadership.

This myth continued as a result of local government management relegating—like information technology development itself—GIS technology to the "dark arts" of the technical "wizards." Often these GIS gurus could not communicate nor demonstrate to decision makers (a) the short-term return on investment in GIS; (b) actual and usable applications for infrastructure development, capital planning, or land use and environmental management, and most importantly; (c) strategic decision making. Not unfairly, the comparison to space exploration—"What is the benefit?" critics say—is *apropos*.

As local government management began to move information technology into its sphere of influence and understand its value as a strategic management tool, however, GIS emerged as a comprehensive information management system. Not only could a GIS integrate all of a local government's data, but it could also overlay county, state, and federal data via the Web.

Today, the sheer power of GIS to easily and quickly analyze and demonstrate the impact of alternative strategies for addressing local challenges makes it a critical tool for local government decision makers. From an internal business perspective, a GIS saves staff time and increases productivity. Its widespread applicability for many different governmental departments and significantly lower costs make it expensive *not* to have GIS.

Having a GIS is an integral part of the technology infrastructure needed for a community to be competitive in attracting new business and industry. Whether it is featuring the attributes of available commercial properties on a Web site for easy access or having permitting systems in place to help speed construction, a GIS will quickly demonstrate its long-term value.

Myth #5: GIS is practical only for federal, state, and county agencies, or large urbanized cities that have need of its massive data integration capabilities for macro analysis.

This once was true, because like all emerging technologies, GIS took time to move from the tactical to the practical. However, GIS technology has reached a point of practicality for most local governments. Residents, no matter what size their community, expect to have the same type of service from their local government as they receive from any business. Given the competitive nature of today's economic climate, the incredible capacity of a GIS to improve service delivery makes it a prudent investment. The "silo" nature of many local governments and the parochialism of political and professional leadership are often greater obstacles to GIS development than the technical and financial constraints. The tools, the data, and the technological expertise is available at lower cost than it has ever been, and the very nature of technological development has been to make the unattainable attainable and apply it to everyday life.

It takes political will to apply this important new technology to everyday business operations, to change and streamline governmental processes and practices, and to move from tactical to practical applications for municipal decision making and governance. According to Gartner, Inc., a Connecticut technology research firm, the demand for GIS will only continue to grow (Robinson 2002). This demand is being driven by GIS working as a comprehensive enterprise, producing data, maps, and applications for all governmental areas of service.

In the end, the myths of GIS—as with all things new, and particularly as seen in local government over the past several decades of major technological development—are in reality the excuses to resist change, both in thinking and in doing business. But change always comes. The choice is in how to approach change.

Consider the example of Burt Rutan. In 2004, Rutan's company, Scaled Composites, successfully launched the first privately funded manned space vehicle, SpaceShipOne, and won the prestigious $10 million Ansari X Prize® for jumpstarting space tourism. An experienced aircraft designer with forty individual designs to his credit, Rutan turned his attention to the problem of manned space flight after becoming "fed up waiting for someone else to take him to space" (Twist 2004). Rutan managed to accomplish in two years what decades of government-funded efforts had failed to achieve—a prototype replacement for the space shuttle.

Local governments often attempt to solve challenges of GIS implementation by focusing on its complexities instead of its possibilities. Burt Rutan focused on the possibilities to launch SpaceShipOne. Building on the experience of the past one hundred years of flight, and much like the Wright Brothers, his innovation and willingness to take the risk triumphed. The technology that Rutan used in designing SpaceShipOne has been available for many years, but he is using it in a much more efficient way (Twist 2004). The lesson for local governments is to look past the challenges that come with change and simply do it.

GIS realities

GIS has forced many local governments to face some hard realities, which up to now were a bit foreign to how business was normally done. Local government functions as a basic model for how governance works in a representative democracy; it represents democracy in action and the ability to determine a community's future. At the same time, local government also serves as a prime example of what does not work well in that governance model, namely a slowness to act due to the need for deliberation and debate. The very nature of a community's ability to govern its own destiny is often at odds with local government's inbred resistance to change and adaptation to the larger world around it. That resistance stems largely from a lack of information available to make informed decisions and be confident about how those decisions impact the community's quality of life.

GIS provides an integrated means to assess geographical data within the community. Regional, state, and national data can also affect all aspects of a community's geopolitical position. GIS can better connect the community with its own resources as well as the larger world in whole new ways. For example, with the power of a GIS, local authorities can draft emergency management plans that provide fire departments with structural building schematics, locations of fire hydrants, sources of combustible materials in the area, and demographics of neighborhood residents. Using up-to-date information on roads and utilities, the fire department can also plan faster routes to save lives and property.

But how can these realities lead to a cost-effective and value-added GIS system? There are a number of strategies local governments can adopt.

1. Cost-effective Web-based data access: GIS has emerged as an important component of the online services being developed by government agencies in large part because it pulls together information from the separate governmental silos across the country. As Jim Geringer, a former governor of Wyoming, said, "GIS should be considered for this initiative as being a parallel to the role e-mail played in the development of the Internet" (Robinson 2002).

Web-based GIS is becoming more and more prevalent. The Web is a useful tool for gathering and manipulating information from a variety of sources. The same is true for GIS information. In the early days of GIS, municipalities needed to buy an expensive software package and multiple licenses to use and manipulate the data needed for a GIS. Today, such purchases are not necessary. With the advent of Java™-based programming,[3] software applications for Web-based GIS work are readily available. Some of these programs require the user to buy software, and others require plug-ins[4] to be added to Web browsers. Many require no special software additions at all and use only the capabilities of existing Web browsers. Because of these advancements, many people who were not able to easily get information now have it at their fingertips. People interested in gathering information find it easily accessible. For the first time, the public can examine the same information as the policy makers.

With Internet connections becoming faster and faster, the amount of information that can be easily transferred is staggering. That is important both in terms of the accessibility and transfer of the datasets as well as the enormous size of digital maps. As a result, municipal, county, state, or federal government agencies can share their analysis of data faster and more efficiently, especially when the information is Web-based.

2. Shared data and data warehousing: *Litera scripta manet*, goes the phrase in Latin ("Words may pass away and be forgotten, but that which is committed to writing will remain as evidence"). A data warehouse model establishes a central repository for GIS data and provides easy access for all users. The model uses GIS as the core technology and is embedded within the existing information technology (IT) infrastructure. It relies on a well-designed central database stored in a relational database management system. The benefits of such an approach are multiple:

a. *Data integrity and quality.* It ensures that data is consistent, accurate, and reliable.
b. *Easy integration and process automation.* It maximizes existing hardware, software, data, and staff to manage, locate, and document GIS data across the enterprise.
c. *Cost-effectiveness and higher productivity.* It allows GIS users to manipulate information on their own, freeing IT staff to focus on running operational systems.
d. *Consistent data.* It provides a single real-time GIS data image for the entire organization.
e. *Better decision making.* Data warehousing contains a history of past events, providing for trend analysis and other types of decision-making processes.

Such an arrangement saves money by eliminating redundant data maintenance, coordinating GIS application development, sharing resources, and gaining efficiency in employee productivity. This enterprise approach is important because 60–80 percent of the cost of GIS implementation is developing and maintaining the GIS digital database. Developing common databases among jurisdictions, or at minimum, separate databases that use a common data model, simply makes economic sense (Integrated Geosciences, Inc. 1998)

Data sharing in Westchester County, New York

Established in 1988, Westchester County GIS has long been a supporter of government data-sharing programs. Recognizing that data development is the single most costly component in building and maintaining a GIS program, Westchester County GIS has successfully demonstrated the significant financial benefits of data sharing to avoid costly and unnecessary duplication.

With early programs focusing on distribution of data through the mail on diskettes or similar media, the county data sharing has evolved into a Web-based program that provides free online access to both non-sensitive spatial datasets and accompanying metadata at the county's GIS Web site *(giswww.westchestergov. com)*. The county has integrated these same datasets as well as Web mapping services into the federal Geospatial One-Stop (GOS) Program.

The foundation of the current Westchester County data-sharing program is the GIS Data Sharing Inter-municipal Agreement (IMA), which was drafted in conjunction with the county attorney's office. The IMA provides a framework that provides data free of charge to local governments in exchange for their datasets. The IMA specifies the intended uses of the data being exchanged, transfer media, required source notes, metadata, and other contact information. Data being requested in or around designated sensitive areas requires approval from the Westchester County Department of Public Safety. While signatures are exchanged between the two participating organizations, no fees are charged or exchanged.

Over the course of seventeen years, Westchester County has found that organizations that collaborate and participate in similar data-sharing agreements are generally very good stewards of data developed—and paid for—from another source. Such informal but structured data-sharing programs can serve as a model to other government programs throughout the country.

Based on materials from Westchester County N.Y.

3. Joint municipal/public-private leveraged development: With increased competition among municipal departments for general fund money, most small- to medium-sized municipal jurisdictions lack either enterprise funding for IT departments or public technology levy initiatives. As a result, GIS is often designated as a long-term but not strategic goal for many IT plans. The strategic mistake in taking this approach is that GIS is the major data integrator for an enterprise system and data warehousing model. For numerous governmental departments, municipal jurisdictions, and public-private agencies, the true but hidden cost is the development and maintenance of databases being duplicated up and down the local government jurisdictional hierarchy. Long-term, such a strategy is enormously detrimental because it wastes public dollars for technology.

4. Integration of departmental address-based functions: Databases of one type or another exist in nearly every local government department, and most have some type of geographical or address element incorporated in them. A GIS has a universal function as the data integrator of all departmental databases that use address-based information. Adopting this strategy enables a GIS to be used "as a method to overlay and combine diverse kinds of data into a single map summarizing geographic, cultural, and scientific attributes. . . defined simplistically, (it) is a computer system capable of holding and using data describing places on the earth's surface" (Matsunaga and Dangermond 1995). From street centerline data to crime statistics analysis, from permit information on a given property to stream bank erosion trends, or from new fire station location in relationship to building types and response times, GIS is an "intelligent mapping system" (ESRI White Paper Series 1993) seamlessly integrating map or graphic data with attribute or tabular data.

Integrating these various departmental address-based functions greatly enhances the usefulness of a GIS, allowing data to be used for multiple purposes. For example, emergency management service data on the type and location of service calls could be used in conjunction with data from the public health department to analyze community health trends. Tying together such diverse data sources into the different layers of a GIS permits not only an interrelational analysis, but more importantly, the ability to illustrate those interrelationships in a digital, three-dimensional thematic map. Such maps have a huge advantage in that they can be modeled and queried by multiple departments in real time, providing a fast and strategic assessment of complex issues.

5. All-encompassing decision-making tool: Strategic assessments are essential in today's fast-paced and dangerous world. GIS provides local government with a decision-making and planning tool that is second to none. Especially when faced with emergency situations, a GIS can produce in-depth analyses and project possible consequences of alternative decisions even as those decisions are being made. Recent headlines point to the usefulness and speed with which GIS can aid decision makers.

In 2004, four powerfully destructive hurricanes hit the state of Florida. GIS played a critical role in preparing for and responding to this string of seemingly unending emergencies. Prior to the storms hitting land, GIS helped with damage assessment and prediction modeling. Immediately after the hurricanes made landfall, GIS assisted with search and rescue operations as well as asset management and staging. During the long-term recovery phase, GIS has had an ongoing role in disseminating information to everyone (*GeoWorld* 2004). This decision making at every phase of the disaster, from preparation to recovery, makes a life-saving difference.

Rishi Sood, an analyst with Gartner, Inc., put it this way, "GIS has always been viewed as something important to some core business functions of government, though not all agencies felt they [needed] it. But since September 11, with the requirements that disaster recovery and security are putting on all agencies in government, there's a growing understanding of GIS as an enterprise application" (Robinson 2002).

Mapping success for a GIS

The benefits of a GIS are readily apparent, but the process for guiding a successful implementation of a GIS does require some thought. The diagram on the following page from the City of Issaquah, Washington, maps out a decision-making process for local government officials and identifies key components for developing a GIS. The steps identified are generic in nature and should be adapted to each local government based on organizational culture and needs.

Key strategies for any tactical plan to facilitate a successful GIS include the following:

- **Involve management.** Local government—elected officials and managers alike—must take a more active role than just providing money and resources. Managers need to help develop organizational strategies for crossing internal departmental "turf" boundaries and actively promote cooperation and collaboration in data sharing and acquisition.
- **Provide ongoing GIS training and education.** Both management and staff need to keep current in GIS technology and applications, particularly as it relates to their disciplines. While GIS is an extraordinarily powerful tool, its value is limited if people do not use it because they do not understand it or are uncomfortable operating it.
- **Continue to promote the benefits of GIS.** Elected leaders especially need to hear about GIS benefits, even after it has been adopted, to ensure continued financial and political support. GIS projects should demonstrate high-quality products and value. High-profile projects with relevance to current information needs often gain public support. The use of GIS for election information and coverage is a prime example.
- **Respond quickly to identified priorities.** GIS projects cannot take years to complete. They must be responsive to users' needs by continuing to explore new ways to make GIS quick and efficient to use, while providing users with easy-to-understand interfaces and task automation.

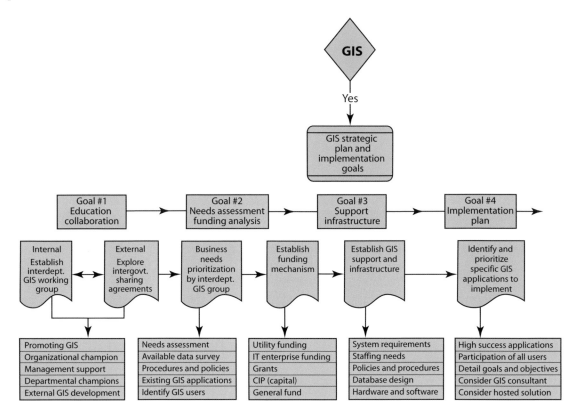

Figure 2.1   Identifying key goals and establishing how decisions will be made for the operations of a local government GIS are critical for ensuring its long-term success. The City of Issaquah, Washington, established this decision tree to help guide the development of its GIS program.

Source: Bill McGill, former Information and Administrative Services Director, City of Issaquah.

- **Communicate, communicate, communicate.** GIS plans must be implemented with frequent progress updates, measured against agreed-upon check points, and given periodic reviews to ensure controlled management and continued support. Clear, nontechnical communication will make a difference in the ultimate success of a GIS.

The procedures presented here should serve as guides for developing a GIS and not be seen as a cookbook recipe that must be rigorously followed. (In chapter 3, Barry Waite provides more detailed advice on implementing a local government GIS.) Each of the major tasks in the GIS development process, and the information generated through the task, should be addressed in any specific project. The methods and forms in this series can be used, or alternatives can be developed, as appropriate to the situation. Keep in mind that a GIS plan is a document to communicate user needs to a GIS analyst. As such, the components of the plan must contain

- descriptions of applications the user can understand
- a logical translation of user requirements to system specifications
- detailed specification suitable for system development

Following the recommendations in the guidelines cannot, unfortunately, guarantee success. Many of the factors outside the control of the GIS development team will affect the ultimate success of the GIS with the definition of success being determined by satisfied GIS users. However, attempting to develop a GIS without following these guidelines, or similar procedures, substantially raises the probability of an unsuccessful GIS project, either one that is not useful or one that substantially exceeds both cost and development time estimates.

Finally, although presented here as an independent activity, GIS development must recognize and interface with other computer systems in local government, such as police and fire dispatch, and facilities management systems, to name a few examples. The GIS must not be viewed as independent of the other systems, but integrated with them to form a true corporate database for local government (Research Foundation of the State University of New York 1996).

In-depth case study by Cory Fleming
eCityGov Alliance, Washington

Profile—regional partnership	
Location	West Central Washington
Size (miles square)	2,200 square miles (King County)
Population	Range from 5,110 to 116,500 (see below)
Form of government	Two-thirds of the communities operate under council-manager; one-third under mayor-council
Annual GIS operating budget	$50,000 initial implementation $28,000 per year maintenance
Number of employees in GIS unit	0.75 FTE

Charter members of the eCityGov Alliance (2004 populations)

Bellevue	116,500
Bothell	30,930
Issaquah	15,510
Kenmore	19,170
Kirkland	45,800
Mercer Island	21,830
Sammamish	35,560
Snoqualmie	5,110
Woodinville	9,915

Overview

King County, Washington, home to the communities participating in the eCityGov Alliance, has a mixture of very urban and very rural areas. GIS applications were introduced to the alliance's portfolio of services in June, 2004. This case study discusses the benefits of collaboration as a means for small communities to establish a GIS program.

Background

King County has thirty-nine municipalities within its borders. The majority are small communities with populations of less than 50,000 and without large budgets. As a result, the communities have developed a tradition of working cooperatively to achieve the necessary economies of scale to offer services and programs that most could not afford to provide to their citizens independently.

In 2001, nine communities put this tradition to work for them by creating the eCityGov Alliance to provide online services to their respective residents. The region is steeped in technology with the Microsoft Corporation headquarters located in Redmond, Washington. Area residents are highly educated and very technologically savvy. The alliance offered the local governments an important means for getting out ahead of the curve and responding to the needs of their citizens. Connie Marshall, mayor of Bellevue, put it this way: "Government always seems to be last in new innovations and new technology. It has a reputation for using an eight-track player when everyone else is using a DVD. This effort gave the local governments a way to be relevant, to be on the cutting edge, to be leading the revolution rather than tagging along from behind."

In-depth case study
eCityGov Alliance, Washington (cont.)

GIS applications became a part of the alliance's portfolio of online services as a result of a downturn in the regional economy. The City of Bellevue, Washington, a charter member of the alliance, began searching for ways to encourage more economic growth in the community. One strategy Bellevue explored was a GIS application to promote commercial real estate sales. While researching the feasibility of the application, Bellevue found that office property site selectors and commercial real estate brokers were not interested in city-specific information, but instead wanted to know what properties were available throughout the region. The city brought the concept to the alliance membership, which decided to purchase the GIS application and make it a part of the portfolio of online services.

Known as *NWProperty.net*, the application provides a comprehensive listing of commercial property for sale and lease, demographic reports, and other public data. The application combines mapping information with tabular data to easily produce a presentation quality report. Potential buyers have instantaneous access to information that a few years ago would have taken them several days to collect. The alliance brought the application online in "an ultra cost-effective manner," said John Backman, executive director of the eCityGov Alliance. "The entire application only cost about $50,000 for nine cities. For the small cities, they got something they never could afford to do on their own." Beyond being a joint effort among the communities in the region, the site is also a public-private partnership with the Commercial Brokers Association, which has responsibility for maintaining the property data. The alliance pays a small fee to access "live" association data.

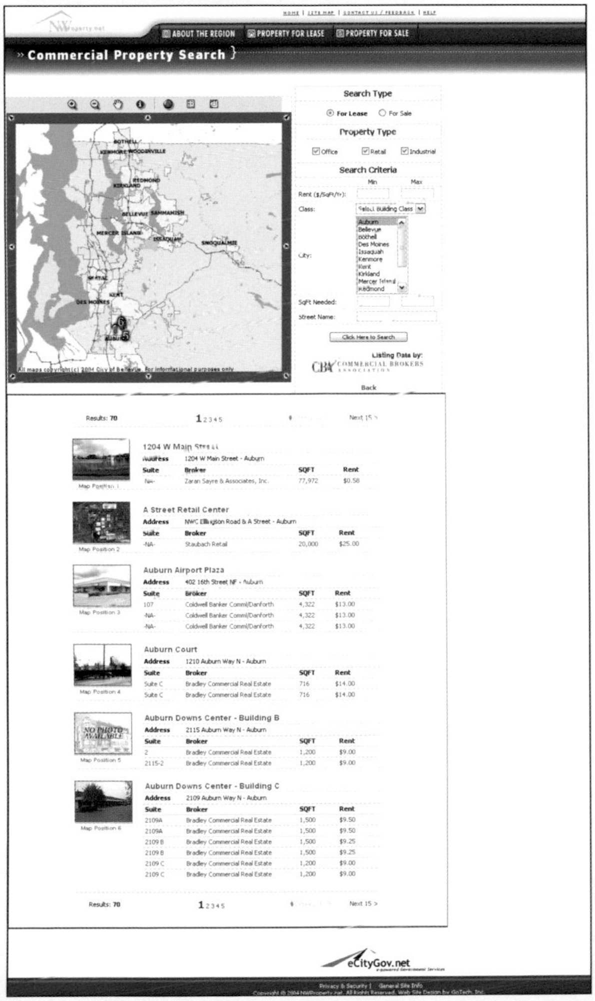

Figure 2.2 The eCityGov Alliance's NWProperty.net uses GIS technology to provide global, national, and local exposure of available commercial properties in the region.

Source: City of Bellevue 2004

eCityGov Alliance, Washington (cont.)

The popularity of the site led the group to explore other potential GIS applications. The latest GIS application provides general community information and enables residents in the region to access a wide variety of public information. For example, a resident can call up community plans for neighborhood enhancements to see what projects might be proposed for his neighborhood. Or a new homeowner can find out where the nearest fire station is for her property insurance. Likewise, residents can access maps of the community's trail systems or learn their property's current assessment. The price tag for the new browser was fairly inexpensive because it used much of the programming code originally developed for the *NWProperty.net* site.

The alliance also made plans to integrate the underlying GIS technology in its other Web-based applications. *MyBuildingPermit.com* and *MyParksandRecreation.com* use GIS components for property searches, maps, and address verification. The ability to reuse GIS components in other applications represents a significant savings in terms of code development and reduced data-maintenance costs.

Concerns and challenges

The cost of the GIS system was a particular concern to the policy makers interviewed. While the investment was not overly expensive, the policy makers reported that they wanted to make sure the community received a good value and the system did not become a "black hole." One city council had no experience in the information technology (IT) field, so did not even know what questions to ask. To address these concerns, IT staff involved in the effort worked hard to present information in plain English and gave demonstrations of the technology whenever possible.

Quantifying the benefits of an application focused at an external user community has been challenging, but local commercial property brokers have expressed their excitement about the project. *NWProperty.net* offers jurisdictional tools such as zoning and land use, property lines, aerial photographs, demographics, crime statistics, and business data. "This additional information is provided in a one-stop shopping format

Figure 2.3   An interactive query function in *NWProperty.net* allows users to pull up available commercial properties based on user-defined criteria.

Source: City of Bellevue 2004

that the other databases do not offer," said Ann Bishop from Investments & Leasing, Wallace Properties, Inc. in Bellevue. "*NWProperty.net* is one of the best commercial property research tools in the market."

On another front, Rich Conrad, city manager of Mercer Island and board chair for the alliance, noted one of the chief benefits of this system—the collective approach the communities took—was also one of the chief hurdles. Each municipality has slightly different processes or systems for daily operations. Before the details of a GIS application can be developed, teams from the different jurisdictions have to agree upon the protocols and processes they all will use to produce one consistent application. To benefit end users, the system must be seamless and easy to use. With a clear goal in place, it is much easier for the project teams to achieve the technical and business process alignments needed.

However, this challenge also provides an excellent opportunity to improve on systems that may have become outdated or irrelevant over time. "You can use the implementation of the technology to review the processes, and reengineer them in a way that makes sense. In this case, [the effort] simply went across city boundaries," said Conrad.

Impact on local government and community

The great variety of potential GIS applications is definitely changing the way local governments operate in the region. Conrad drew a parallel between GIS data and financial data. Just as most local governments have moved their financial systems from paper accounting to an electronic format, geographical data must ultimately be moved to a computerized system. Most city functions involve finances, which have to be tracked and managed carefully, said Conrad. "We've had automated systems for handling financial data for decades," he said. "Almost everything else a city does has a geographic component to it. . . ..We need to automate that type of information and put in the hands of the employees who deal with it every day."

For a small community undergoing tremendous growth, GIS presents a means for meeting the city's daily operational needs without having to vastly increase staff size. Fuzzy Fletcher, mayor of Snoqualmie, and Bob Larson, city administrator, saw the potential of GIS to impact a number of operational issues, from building permits to utilities to fleet management and much more. They agreed Snoqualmie would have to hire another half a dozen staff members if the city did not have access to GIS technology.

Mayor Marshall said the Bellevue City Council wanted to give city staff new challenges and more exciting things to do. The council sought to maximize staff capabilities and energize employees by transitioning more mundane tasks to the GIS. "The city gained new efficiencies, but not at the expense of human bodies. Many staff were retrained and work in new areas," she said.

The added value of GIS data is that not only can city employees use it to improve the quality and delivery of city services, but the general public can also make use of the data. Marshall said the work of city government is much more transparent to residents who can compare what's happening in their neighborhood with other neighborhoods. "Putting our historical data online is especially important because residents can see that over time and realize that the investment in all the neighborhoods is about the same. It may not be even, but it is fair," said Marshall.

Involvement of local government officials

Chief executive officers (CEOs), either the mayor or the city manager, need to be involved in implementing a GIS. Their job, in large part, is to champion the cause and sell the idea to the city council. Mayor Marshall said they also have to direct traffic, so they need to understand the utility of the effort. Rich Conrad observed that most of the risk-taking will be done by these individuals, so their involvement is imperative. "There will be tough decision-making points along the way, and the mayor or manager better know about those before the decision is needed," he said.

Benefits of GIS

Members of eCityGov Alliance want to take advantage of the unique nature of a GIS, and its large number of potential uses. Members are looking for the best ways to leverage existing assets—public data they have been collecting for many years—and make that information available for both internal users and the general public. The Snoqualmie officials, Mayor Fletcher and Bob Larson, pointed out that their community has a tremendous need for accurate maps that can be produced quickly and with many different types of information. They noted that a few years ago if the city needed to install a new sewer, it had to hire a civil engineering firm to survey the area and produce a map. It was expensive and time-consuming. With that information available digitally through a GIS, the time and money saved offers huge benefits for their municipality.

Governance model

The GIS applications used by the alliance are not seen as particularly unique by the group. They recognize many other communities across the country have similar applications. What they say is unique about their effort is the governance model they adopted. According to Conrad, the alliance "represents shared risks and benefits. The communities have real ownership—technically, financially, and organizationally—in the alliance." Fletcher and Larson reported it has been very beneficial for their community to get in on the ground floor of the alliance. They have been able to bring their community's needs to the group, help set priorities, and grow with the GIS.

Managing the alliance's many projects is not without challenges and relies heavily on both the formal structure and the informal personnel connections of board members, project leaders, and team members. The alliance is overseen by an executive board made up of city managers and administrators. Meeting on a quarterly basis, this group sets the policies for the alliance. The operations board is made up of assistant city managers and department heads. This group meets more frequently—on a monthly basis—to oversee projects, monitor the budget, and help prioritize workloads. At the project level, each application has a multicity project team with a self-selected project leader. Depending on the size of the application, numerous subteams working in more specialized areas may also be formed. Daily operations of the alliance have the oversight of an executive director, a full-time equivalent staff position funded by the alliance partners and headquartered in Bellevue, the largest municipality participating in the alliance.

Advice to other local governments

Alliance members recommend researching available options for implementing a GIS. Fletcher and Larson encouraged local government officials to look at a proposed GIS and consider the financial implications thoroughly. They noted that with all the potential applications offered by a GIS, the investment likely would be worth the risks.

Rich Conrad also urged community leaders to talk to others about their experiences and, when possible, to work jointly with other governments. "There will be benefits you can't predict until you've gotten into using the system," he said. For example, while inventorying Mercer Island's infrastructure via GPS field surveys, city officials found pipes, drains, and other infrastructure they did not know existed. Similarly, since GIS databases are address-based, implementing a GIS forces a city to resolve conflicts or ambiguities in street addresses. This helps public works and public safety employees to improve customer service and emergency response times.

Finally, GIS is becoming less expensive. As Mayor Marshall put it, "If the city budget is hurting, then your customers are hurting, too. Keeping taxes low is important when the economy is in a slump. However, you still have to maintain the quality of city services." A shared GIS like that developed by the eCityGov Alliance can help cities provide critical services to residents without overburdening their employees or resources.

References

ESRI White Paper Series. 1993. Enterprise GIS: Using GIS in the corporate environment. May. Redlands, Calif.: ESRI.

GeoWorld. 2004. Devastating hurricane season tests Florida emergency response: Interview with Carla Boyce. Available online at www.geoplace.com/uploads/industryinterview/boyce.asp.

Integrated Geoscience, Inc.1998. Final report: Geographical information system implementation plan for the City of Billings, Mont. Markham, Ontario, Canada: Integrated Geoscience Inc.

Macgunigal, Maria, senior GIS Analyst, City of Sacramento, Calif. 1999. As quoted in "A spatial data approach to the social sciences" by Kyle Bohnenstiehl. *GIS Vision*, December.

Mark, David M., et al. 1997. The GIS history project. A paper presented at the University Consortium for Geographic Information Science (UCGIS) 1997 Summer Assembly.

Matsunaga, Keene, and Jack Dangermond. 1995. Promoting a free access or minimal cost of dissemination arrangement for government-held geographic information systems data (Unabridged). Proceedings of the 1995 ESRI User Conference, May 22–26, 1995, in Palm Springs, Calif.

Research Foundation of the State University of New York. 1996. GIS development guide: Manager's overview. Available online at www.geog.buffalo.edu/sara/manager.htm.

Robinson, Brian. 2002. GIS vision fades at local level. Federal Computer Week, May 16, 2002. Available online at www.fcw.com/geb/articles/2002/0513/web-gis-05-16-02.asp.

Sarkar, Dibya. 2003. Local governments use GIS. Federal Computer Week, December 11, 2003. Available online at www.fcw.com/geb/articles/2003/1208/web-gis-12-11-03.asp.

Twist, Jo. 2004. Burt Rutan: Aviation pioneer. BBC News, October 4, 2004. Available online at news.bbc.co.uk/1/hi/sci/tech/3746313.stm.

Zhao, Hongwei. 2002. Using geographic information system (GIS) in local government: A case study of GIS implementation in Ascension Parish, Louisiana. Master's thesis. Baton Rogue, La.: Louisiana State University, Department of Architecture.

Notes

1. William McGill died on March 31, 2005, during the final stages of the preparation of this manuscript. He was retired at the time of his death.

2. The Geospatial One-Stop System is a federal project to help facilitate a collaborative effort to collect and share geographic data among federal, state, and local governments.

3. Java is a general purpose programming language with a number of features that make the language well suited for use on the Web. Small Java applications are called Java applets and can be downloaded from a Web server and run on a personal computer by a Java-compatible Web browser, such as Netscape Navigator or Microsoft Internet Explorer.

4. A hardware or software module that adds a specific feature or service to a larger system. The idea is that the new component simply plugs in to the existing system. For example, there are number of plug-ins for the Netscape Navigator browser that enable it to display different types of audio or video messages. Navigator plug-ins are based on MIME file types.

3

Planning, implementing, and funding a GIS

Barry Waite
GIS Administrator, City of Carson, California

Many people hesitate to get started in GIS. They have heard stories about exorbitant costs or failed efforts. They fear getting in over their heads, starting a program they will not be able to control. In fact, any community can implement a GIS. It is not a risky venture. It is a well-accepted part of local government operations across the country in communities large and small.

Other chapters in this book answer the questions of why communities should have a GIS and how to use it. This chapter describes some real-world suggestions for

- developing a plan
- getting started
- selecting hardware and software
- securing and maintaining data
- staffing
- paying for GIS
- avoiding mistakes

While no item here applies to every community, and what works in one location may not work in another, this chapter provides ideas to help get a community started and avoid some common pitfalls. Readers should feel free to use ideas that will work in their community and discard the rest.

Developing a plan

A geographic information system must begin with a detailed implementation plan that describes the collection and accuracy levels of data, models for the data, the applications for each person in the organization, job descriptions, and a five-year funding plan. Or, at least many local government officials believe they must have these details worked out before they can get started, and they see that as an unattainable goal. But developing a GIS plan is not such a formidable undertaking if the work is broken down into well-defined tasks.

Organizational support

New technology programs require a champion within each organization, and GIS is no exception. This person promotes the system within the agency, company, or entity and lobbies for resources. The most important qualifications for the champion are enthusiasm and access to decision makers. A good place to find such a person is to look in the mirror. Someone interested in reading this book may be just the person to take up the cause.

Another key player is a project manager, who often functions as a champion. The project manager will handle the organizational side of GIS, while the champion serves as a cheerleader. If two people fill these roles, they will divide tasks according to their abilities, knowledge, and positions in the organization.

Involving potential users and other people from different parts of an organization will help broaden support for the GIS. It may also lead to an enterprise system, a GIS that serves and connects multiple divisions within an organization. These individuals can form a user group to guide the planning and implementation of the system. They can also seek support from senior management and elected officials. The user group can be an ongoing part of any GIS program, providing overall guidance and encouraging an exchange of ideas and resources. To develop a successful user group, the champion or project manager should

- form the user group early in the implementation process
- make sure the members know they have the backing of upper management, even if that backing is only for an exploratory effort
- keep both the user group and management informed as the process moves forward to help ensure their continuing support

A user group need not have a formal structure. It can serve as a forum for seeking solutions to shared problems. In some cases, the group acts as a steering committee, setting policy and allocating resources. In other cases, it is an informal and occasional gathering of employees who use GIS or whose work is impacted by GIS. Either type of group can help develop a plan for a GIS. Some previously unenthusiastic staff members may get excited over a new GIS application when given the opportunity to innovate and have an impact on the organization. In the long run, those previous skeptics can become the biggest supporters of GIS.

The planning process needs people from all levels of an organization. But as with any information technology project, a new system can cause concern among some employees. Their involvement early on gives them a better understanding of what GIS can do and how it will impact them. If they have a voice in developing the plan, they will be more supportive in implementing and maintaining the system. Thus, directors and line workers can all contribute to assure the plan is comprehensive.

Needs assessment

An assessment interview often goes something like this:

Project manager: "What are your GIS needs?"
Staff member: "Well, I don't know. What can GIS do for me?"
Project manager: "Well, what do you need it do?"
Staff member: "I'm not sure. What can it do?"

It is unfair to expect people to describe how they plan to use a tool that they only vaguely understand. Introducing them to the potential benefits of a GIS before a needs assessment can help move the process along. For example, a GIS Day event—complete with explanations of how GIS works and examples of what it can do—would be an excellent kickoff. There are many resources available online at *www.gisday.com*, including posters and other documents that do not require any GIS software to reproduce. While the official GIS Day is held in November each year to coincide with Geography Awareness Week, a local event can be scheduled at any convenient time. If projects, or better yet GIS staff members, from neighboring communities are available, they can explain real applications for solving problems in the region.

The City of Torrance, California, puts on a large annual expo—complete with classes and presentations—for city staff and the community to better understand GIS and use the tools available. East of Torrance, the City of Carson has maps about current issues simply displayed in the lobby of city hall. A community just getting started with GIS can use the same approach to educate the organization. An event can be as simple or complex as desired, and can be a one-time occasion or an annual program for selected staff or the entire community. Another useful way to educate people on the benefits of GIS is to distribute ESRI publications, including *ArcUser*™, the quarterly magazine aimed at software users, and *Government Matters*, the quarterly newsletter that describes how government uses GIS. In any case, an educational effort beforehand will make for a much more effective needs assessment.

To identify some of the more important uses of GIS, think about the community's most pressing issues and how GIS might address them. In one city, vacant commercial buildings were eyesores and generated little revenue to pay for city services. The city created an Internet-based GIS application to market these properties for redevelopment and reuse. Another small town had a problem with water main easements that were not properly recorded. Converting the old drawings and combining them with digital parcels made it easy to check the parcel records and identify missing easements. Thinking about specific projects makes it easier to define information and resources that a GIS can provide.

If an organization has a formal work plan or written goals, the GIS needs assessment should dovetail with those goals. Once goals are defined, GIS could help with the highest priorities. It can also help in the opposite direction. In one city, the community-wide goals had not been updated in several years and no longer clearly reflected local concerns or the issues facing each department. Developing a GIS plan allowed the community to address its needs in a comprehensive fashion. The effort brought together people from different departments to discuss similar issues and the impact of plans. While many of the items were only tangentially related to GIS, the result was a new set of goals that addressed the city's most pressing issues and a GIS plan to help meet those goals.

A needs assessment or analysis can be very important to set the direction for the program and create a long-term plan. It will stir-up interest and encourage discussion. However, analyzing needs is one of the most difficult parts of the planning process because most people will not know how GIS can help them do their jobs.

While it would certainly be desirable to identify every need at the planning stage, the reality is many needs are not immediately evident. And GIS technology will inevitably evolve to address problems that cannot be addressed immediately. New problems will arise, or the state or federal governments will impose new regulations. The needs assessment is an evolving document and, if regularly updated, can serve as a planning tool.

Consultants

If employees do not have the background or time to conduct an assessment in-house, a consultant may fill the void. But hiring a consultant has its pros and cons. For some organizations, an outside expert may be able to gain credibility with decision makers that staff lacks. Consultants know what starting a GIS involves and can share the experiences from a number of agencies. A consultant can generally complete an assessment more quickly than in-house personnel, who have to take time away from their regular duties. However, consultants can be expensive, and hiring a consultant may take longer than the assessment itself depending on local procurement rules. Finally, some consultants may have a boilerplate plan they follow with every organization, or they may use the needs assessment as an opportunity to sell their own products.

A simple check of past projects can avoid most problems with consultants:

- Check with a consultant's references. Call other clients to ask how the process went for them and if they felt using a consultant had provided good value for the money.
- Ask how well the consultant stayed on schedule, recognizing that schedules slip because of the client's actions as often as the consultant's. Make a point to find out why a project fell behind schedule or how the project managed to stay on schedule. Learning from others' mistakes and successes can help develop a plan that works.
- Review another community's request for proposals (RFP) to help determine what qualities to look for in a potential consultant.

A consultant can help the organization define its needs and GIS priorities as well as its overall goals and objectives. There may be projects that would be very useful but require data that either does not exist or is not cost-effective to gather. Certain projects may require technical expertise beyond the staff's abilities. Specialized hardware may not be affordable. In other cases, a project comes up that will be difficult but is important enough to tackle right away. Also, some very high priorities must follow lower priority projects because of relationships between projects. For example, marketing vacant properties may be a higher priority than creating zoning maps, but since zoning is part of the marketing effort, creating the maps needs to precede the marketing effort.

One final note on using consultants to conduct a needs assessment: if possible, have the consultant lead staff through the process instead of doing all the work. The result will be a product that the organization owns instead of one regarded as an outsider's work.

Resources and constraints

After completing the needs assessment, identify the available resources and constraints. Drafting technicians, who can be retrained for GIS work, are a resource. A water agency that already has all its water lines in a CAD (computer-assisted design) system—and will share the information—is a resource. Parcel lines that exist only on old and poor-quality paper maps are a constraint. In an organizational analysis, resources and constraints may also be called opportunities and threats. They can point out available funding, staff, information, or equipment while warning of problems such as privacy issues, political pitfalls, or a lack of information infrastructure.

Developing a timeline to show the GIS implementation schedule helps communicate priorities to management and staff. A timeline shows when each item is expected to be completed or available for use. For example, a timeline would show that census data might be available two months after start-up. Creating parcels may take several months. An off-the-shelf application may be available within a few weeks, and another may take months to customize for a special purpose. Many GIS plans offer to do all things right away. Unless the plan includes hiring out the entire effort to a large and highly competent consulting firm and paying a huge premium,

ID	Task Name	Start	End	Duration	May 2005			Jun 2005			Jul 2005				Aug 2005		
					5/8	5/15	5/22	5/29	6/5	6/12	6/19	6/26	7/3	7/10	7/17	7/24	7/31	8/7	8/14	8/21
1	Create base data	5/9/2005	6/30/2005	7.80w													
2	Parcels	5/9/2005	6/17/2005	6w													
3	Obtain parcels from county	5/9/2005	6/9/2005	4.80w													
4	Clean up parcels and connect ownership data	6/9/2005	6/17/2005	1.40w													
5	Aerial photos	5/9/2005	5/23/2005	2.20w													
6	Download USGS and project them	5/9/2005	5/23/2005	2.20w													
7	Streets	6/9/2005	6/30/2005	3.20w													
8	Download Census TIGER files and adjust with aerial photos	6/9/2005	6/30/2005	3.20w													
9	Applications	6/30/2005	8/1/2005	4.60w													
10	Print basic street map	6/30/2005	7/7/2005	1.20w													
11	Create zoning map	7/11/2005	8/1/2005	3.20w													
12	Create water system network from CAD files - pilot area	7/1/2005	8/1/2005	4.40w													

Figure 3.1 Gantt charts, such as this one, can help local government staff and elected officials understand plans for implementing a GIS, including steps to complete a given task.

Source: Barry Waite, City of Carson, Calif.

the result will be competition between users, missed deadlines, and lots of frustration. A Gantt chart *(figure 3.1)* may help people see the order of implementation, the dependency among different projects, and the trade-offs that must occur during implementation.

An open discussion of priorities will help determine what is possible and manage expectations. If someone's favored application is not an initial priority, make that clear and set a projected start time for it. Alternatively, show what steps must take place before the application can begin. Such discussions should also include management staff that will ultimately decide or at least approve the priority listing. While the dynamics of the organization will impact how discussions are organized and decisions made, empowering staff in the process pays big dividends by giving it a stake in the success of the GIS.

In thinking through the priorities in developing a GIS, keep in mind that the system will alter the way the organization does business. This may have an impact on the proposed order for developing new GIS applications. Automating certain tasks such as issuing building permits or generating maps of the city's infrastructure may save a tremendous amount of staff time and eliminate the need to hire new people to work with area developers and contractors. Such a benefit may move the development of a particular GIS application to the top of the priority list.

GIS should make a task easier, not more difficult. Getting to know the totality of a process before designing the GIS makes for a well-integrated system. A good understanding of the existing process shows all the geographic components of it, such as address, parcel number, or intersection, and makes for a more comprehensive solution. Expecting GIS staff members to integrate GIS with a building permit process they don't fully understand will lead to an unending series of changes and workarounds. Process analysis often uncovers areas that have nothing to do with GIS, but the GIS application is a handy excuse to make needed changes. However, the goal should be to have the GIS become an integrated part of the activity instead of a new task. Another important side benefit is the opportunity to encourage greater cooperation between departments. GIS can link many different activities. Traffic volume data is useful to both the traffic engineer and the economic development staff. Demographic data is important to the community planner and the recreation department. When people in the various departments start to see how information can be shared and their activities interrelate, it helps them think about the big picture instead of their narrow work area.

Why do some GIS plans fail? One reason is there is no real plan. A manager gets excited about GIS and buys equipment and software without any idea of what to do with it. Examples include purchasing a large-format scanner with no plan of what to scan or routing software with no plan of what to route. The purchases set the priorities instead of the priorities determining the purchases. While it is not necessary to have a fully detailed plan, starting out with no purpose at all almost certainly dooms a GIS. On the other hand, some towns have spent their entire budget developing a beautiful plan with no money left to do anything. A similar problem occurs when so much time is spent on developing a plan that people lose interest. A generalized plan the organization actually uses is better than a detailed plan that never gets implemented.

Lack of management support has killed many new projects. Keep management sold on the benefits throughout the process. Implementing GIS without information technology support, such as a network, will not lead to success beyond the single-user system. A GIS that connects the enterprise and works across organizational lines needs some basic network infrastructure and support, either from staff or vendors. Finally, trying to use another community's plan will likely fail or at least create a system that does not meet a community's specific needs. Using someone else's plan is like using someone else's X-ray to treat an illness. Learning from their plan can provide useful insight. Adopting it outright is a likely road to trouble.

Why do other GIS plans succeed? They have realistic expectations. They have a plan developed by different levels of the organization addressing local issues. They have support from management. They have information technology support.

By following these steps to create a GIS plan, the organization will have a good sense about the benefits of a GIS. Projects will be lined up, priorities set, and a schedule put in place. None of this will be set in stone. Be flexible as things unfold and update the plan annually to make sure everyone is on the same page and doing what is most important to the organization as a whole. The next section looks at getting started with a GIS program.

Getting started

The phrase, "think globally, act locally," certainly applies to an organization implementing a GIS. Many communities have been successful by starting out with small and well-defined projects and then expanding to serve an entire GIS enterprise. Another way of describing it would be "think big, start small." Think big by considering how the information used in the first projects can be used in the future. Start small by doing one project, one part of the county, one department, or perhaps even just one license for the software.

The "think big" part ensures that decisions for early projects do not constrain the system later. For example, an early project showing park areas may require only simple lot lines, but later uses will require much more precise data such as the location of utilities to within a few inches. If possible, start with the level of precision likely needed for future projects so the investment in getting the information is made just once. On the other hand, do not demand that everything be absolutely precise on the off chance that such a level of precision may be needed someday for some unknown application. A GIS that produces useful information with data recognized to be a few feet off is far better than a GIS with extremely precise data that can never be used because all the effort goes into making it perfect.

The "start small" part keeps the effort manageable and allows people to get their feet wet. Many organizations like to start with a pilot program that is important to the organization but limited in scope. The City of Lakewood, California, started its GIS with a flood zone analysis to remove the flood insurance requirement for many residents. More than 5,100 homeowners saved about $400 per year as a result of the pilot, and the city's GIS was off and running.

Not every organization needs to start out with a single pilot project. After developing a GIS plan, a community may be ready to implement multiple applications at once. In such a case, a pilot project may not be necessary. That is especially true if there are experienced GIS users involved early in the implementation process. A discussion on staffing later in the chapter goes into this subject in more detail. Still, most organizations would be well served to avoid starting off with too many applications at once. There will always be growing pains along with unforeseen opportunities and constraints. Starting smaller makes it easier to take advantage of the opportunities and deal with the constraints.

An organization particularly averse to risk—and there are many risk-averse government agencies—is well served by starting small. Small successes go a long way toward increasing the comfort level of decision makers, setting manageable expectations, and meeting those expectations with relative ease. Some very change-resistant agencies have been successful using this approach.

The first maps produced by any GIS are some of the most exciting, even if they are very simple. A common first map will reproduce zoning areas. Such maps will replace hand-drawn maps that are difficult to change and enormously expensive to reproduce. Make sure to display these early efforts in a conspicuous place to show the new GIS is real and producing something. The sooner they go up on the wall, the better. At the same time, stress that these products are a work in progress and can easily be changed. One of the most common first reactions is that people will not like the colors of the map. Show them how easy it is to change the colors and use different colors for different uses of the same data. While hardly a key benefit of GIS, it gives people something they have not had before—control over how they view and present geographic information.

Selecting software and hardware

Nothing has changed faster and more completely in GIS than the computer software and hardware needed to run it. The days of costly, single-purpose workstations are gone. Meanwhile, the equipment needed to run a GIS has become much more powerful and more affordable. The result has made GIS affordable for a town with two thousand people or a county with eight million.

Software

There are two main types of GIS data work: (1) data creation and editing, and (2) data analysis and output production. To build and edit significant amounts of GIS data requires a robust software package like ArcInfo® or ArcEditor™. Data analysis and output generation can be done with a more general package like ArcView® software, which has cartographic tools, analysis tools, and even some editing tools. Except in larger organizations, one copy of ArcInfo will usually suffice. The bigger question is how many users will need ArcView. Do not put ArcView on any person's desktop untrained to use it. While training certainly need not be extensive and can take the form of classes, online courses, or books, it is not reasonable to expect someone to use the software without training. Like driving a car, GIS software is not difficult to learn but it does require some instruction. Start with ArcView on the computers of those who will be using the first applications that require the software and add more licenses as needed.

One of the biggest changes in using GIS has been the Internet. Many, if not most, people using GIS applications access them through a Web browser. In fact, they may not even know they are using a GIS. Access to parcel information, transit route selection, and marketing of available properties are three common applications. They are easy to use and require no special hardware or software on the part of the user. However, these applications can require more work on the part of staff to develop and maintain. They also require specialized software and a computer server to provide them. But many commercial services provide the applications, and such services will also host them on their computer system. The trade off compared to running the applications on the organization's own system is a potentially less flexible system and higher costs over the long term.

Creating Web-based GIS applications is no longer a difficult undertaking. Several off-the-shelf software packages make creating applications easy to set up and manage. Extensive programming skills are not required, although customized programming can add to the functionality of the applications. Many excellent GIS applications are available, serving hundreds and even thousands of users at a time with a single application.

For smaller applications serving a limited number of people in a few different locations, such as city hall and the city maintenance yard, Web-based GIS applications provide a tremendous economy of scale compared to loading software on numerous computers and updating each of them every time an application or data changes. The City of Carson, California, created a Web-based property information system for its planning department. Planners access the information they need about zoning, property ownership, and permits using a simple Web browser. Systems like this can be open to the public or limited to staff inside the organization. Internal-only GIS applications are referred to as being intranet-based as opposed to those that are Internet-based and open to the general public. Internet applications can have a password function to close all or part of their functionality to the general public. The fact that information can be made so easily available to the public and businesses makes Web-based GIS applications even more attractive.

Web applications need not be high-tech projects. Publishing maps with Adobe® Acrobat® gives anyone access to them with little effort. While the maps are not as interactive as Web applications, they are useful in viewing static information, such as aerial photos or zoning information. As an alternative to the Internet, applications can be distributed on a compact disk for limited distribution of sensitive information like homeland security data.

Another important type of software helps access and manage large multiuser geographic databases. Arc-SDE® is one example of this type of database management system. ArcSDE runs on a server and works with other database systems—like Microsoft SQL Server, Oracle®10g, and Informix® Dynamic server—to access the geographic information stored in them. It acts as the GIS gateway to a relational database. Many organizations already have extensive database systems. Including geographic data in them can be a logical extension of their functionality and provide added value for the GIS. In larger organizations, access to such software may quickly become a necessity for managing large amounts of information. However, when just starting out, most organizations will not need such software until their GIS is more established, if at all.

ESRI has developed more specialized software for functions like business analysis, routing, modeling, and facilities management. Other software developers have created special packages for applications like crime analysis, pavement management, and accident tracking. There is even a program available to assist with cemetery management. These packages make it easy to get started with well-tested applications with a good user interface. Many of them include data and can be used right out of the box. Considering the range of what is currently available, it is clearly a great time to get started in GIS.

Hardware

As computing power goes up and costs drop, hardware purchases are no longer a dominant part of starting a GIS. Disk storage space has become very inexpensive. Even a small town can afford and make use of high-capacity servers. Printers are relatively fast and reliable. Scanners can easily handle projects that would have required very expensive and temperamental equipment a few years ago. Global positioning system (GPS) receivers suitable for some GIS uses are available at the local Kmart. Handheld computers that fit in a shirt pocket hold more power than a personal computer from a decade ago.

Servers and workstations

Some uses require a more expensive GIS computer workstation. Tasks such as classifying vegetation coverage from large areas of aerial photos will take all the computing horsepower available. Even for these types of applications, the cost of a specialized workstation is in the thousands of dollars now, not the twenty thousand from a few years ago. For a person using ArcInfo to create and edit data, a good personal computer with some extra memory should suffice. For other GIS users with ArcView, any modern personal computer should be up to the task. If staff members already have computers purchased in the last year or two for general office use, they will most likely find those computers adequate for their GIS needs.

A GIS uses extraordinarily large databases, which are generally housed on a data server. A data server will likely be one of the most powerful computers on site, running very large databases and serving many users at the same time. However, a data server can also be an ordinary desktop computer for just a few users with read-only access. But using a server instead of a shared drive on a user's computer will provide for a more robust system with less disruption to the users. Costs for a dedicated server can vary from several thousand dollars for a high-end server with a separate data storage array to less than a thousand dollars for a simple desktop computer. Most server solutions require trained professionals to properly configure them and, in some cases, maintain them on a daily basis. Scrimping money on configuration is simply not a good idea in the long run.

Printers

The cost of printers varies dramatically. The most common printer for maps is a desktop inkjet printer making letter-sized maps (8 by 11 inch). These printers are available from many retailers, often for less than $100. A tabloid-sized (11 by 17 inch) map is very useful. It is small enough to use in a vehicle or pass around at a meeting, yet twice as clear as a letter-sized map. Maps of this size can also be produced with an inkjet printer. With any real amount of use, however, the cost of inkjet cartridges will soon make an inexpensive printer seem like less than a bargain.

In general, laser printers are much faster than inkjet printers. Color laser printers have become much more affordable on a cost per page basis and less prone to breakdown than earlier models. Most users prefer the quality of the laser print over an inkjet print. Many tabloid-sized color laser printers are on the market, and these printers can serve as a general purpose printer for an entire office while also serving GIS needs. Although large, color workgroup laser printers can cost several thousand dollars, they also can replace other printers that may be more expensive to maintain and operate in the long run.

Many people associate large-format printers, which used to be known as plotters, with GIS. Not so many years ago, plotters used a number of colored pens that moved across the paper to create an image. Plotting was a lengthy exercise, and reprinting due to simple errors was an expensive annoyance at best. Most recent large-format printers function as large inkjet printers with four or more print heads moving rapidly across the paper. Some even use seven colors of ink for better quality results. Many models have scanners built in to inspect print quality and ensure a proper color match. Most have a built-in paper cutter to automatically cut each map as the paper feeds off a long roll. A 36-inch-wide model is standard for GIS purposes, with 24 by 36 inch being the most common size map. Printing sideways on the paper can make a 36-by-48-inch map. Going beyond that size, the software and hardware usually allow for a tiled effect, printing several sheets that can be assembled into a huge single map. For practical purposes, most people seldom, if ever, make maps larger than 36-by-48 inches.

The price for large-format printers varies more than almost any other piece of GIS equipment. Several affordable light-duty printers that can fit on a desktop exist. The most popular printers used for the vast majority of local government purposes cost about $9,000. They are floor-mounted on a stand and use large tanks of ink holding over 600 milliliters of ink. (In comparison, most desktop inkjet cartridges carry about 40 milliliters.) The result is a very low ink cost per page. The cost for regular use rolls of paper is also low with a total cost per page of only a few dollars for a 24-by-36-inch print. Using glossy or other special papers such as transparencies can drive up the cost notably, as can using special ink designed for long-term outdoor use.

Before making any major purchase, local governments should test out equipment whenever possible. Many vendors provide trial machines to use either in the office or with customer data in their offices. A neighboring community may make their large-format plotters available for experimental purposes, although buying a roll of paper from time to time would probably be appreciated. This provides time to determine how much large-sized printing will be needed on a regular basis and what features are most useful. Keep in mind that this type of on-site printer will be used much more often than an outside printing service because it is convenient and easily accessible. On the other hand, it may also show demand is small enough to use a printing service as needed instead of purchasing equipment. As a general rule, most communities find it cheaper and more convenient to have their own large-format printer.

Scanners

Many paper maps and images can be converted to an electronic format usable in GIS with a scanner. Scanning smaller items requires only a typical office scanner; many good models are available for under $200. Larger items, such as plot plans and maps, require a large-format scanner. As with printers, the cost depends on the speed and features. Some scanners can also work as a plain copier, which can be very useful. Color scanners are significantly more expensive. Typically, local governments purchasing a monochrome scanner will spend about $10,000.

More often, local governments will send out their plans and maps to be scanned by a service. Unless there is a continuing volume of items to scan, using a service can be highly cost-effective. A service can process the scanned images to make them more useful for GIS, such as extracting the specific features like curb lines or pipelines. A hybrid plan is to send out older files to a service bureau and do ongoing scanning in-house as new items come in. The question is how much material there will be and how much either option costs. Local vendors can provide pricing per item to scan, including any added services that might be desired.

Global positioning system (GPS) receivers

Global positioning system (GPS) receivers are a popular tool for GIS. By measuring the time it takes for a signal to reach the receiver from a set of satellites in space, a GPS can determine its position on the ground. Common uses of GPS include mapping infrastructure such as water valves or street signs, or tracking hazardous material spills on public streets. Even more than with printers and scanners, the price of GPS units varies depending on the accuracy and desired features. Handheld units from a local sporting goods store go for $200 and are entirely acceptable for certain uses. They may have an accuracy of twenty-five feet. Survey-grade quality units can cost one hundred times that much, but they are accurate to within one centimeter. Attaching a laser to the receiver will cost about $5,000, but it can speed acquiring data by taking many points from one location. It also has the added benefit of being a much safer way to gather the locations of water valves in the street rather than standing on a highway.

The question is accuracy. What level of accuracy does a given application require? Within a centimeter? A meter? Or ten meters? For locating buildings, low accuracy will do. Someone within twenty feet will certainly find the building. For street trees, being within a few feet will work. For digging around a gas pipeline, fairly close simply will not do. The risk is much too high. If a lower-grade GPS receiver is used for such a situation, it should be made clear that the data is not highly accurate and should not be used for design purposes. Some cities share a midrange GPS receiver since they do not use it daily and can schedule between them conveniently. Universities purchase GPS units and allow their students to do projects for surrounding communities as a training program. There are also many consultants who can quickly inventory various features with GPS at a reasonable rate. Starting out with a consultant gathering some points and then using city staff for ongoing operations may be the most economical solution. Certainly, the low cost of handheld receivers makes them a useful tool in any GIS for the right purpose.

Other equipment

Handheld computers, specifically personal digital assistants (PDAs), are another related technology. With ArcPad® software, a PDA can take the GIS into the field for real-time access to information. Attaching a GPS receiver allows continuous editing using a simple user interface. GPS units that plug directly into a PDA are not as accurate as the somewhat more expensive units that attach by a cable. In the very near future, expect to see maintenance workers using this type of system for tracking their work orders. The cost for a PDA useful for GIS is several hundred dollars, a figure that has not changed much in the last few years. The power of the equipment for that price, however, continues to rise quickly. More expensive "rugged-ized" PDAs are available for heavy field use and all-weather situations. Also, special carrying cases that will make any PDA more rugged are available for a much lower cost.

Thoughts on purchasing

In GIS, bundling hardware and software can provide excellent values for the buyer. Offers found on the ESRI Web site, for example, include ArcPad with a PDA, scanners with scanning software, high-end computers with ArcInfo, and large-format printers with ArcPress™ software. Vendors usually have additional offers, so it pays to look around for them before buying hardware and software separately.

A common mistake is to buy hardware and software before they are needed. Technology does not age well, so there is no point in buying something that will sit in the carton for months. Do not purchase a workstation in May for a project that will not likely start until December. Worse yet, priorities may change, and the new priorities may need different software or equipment. Buying on an as-needed basis reduces the risk.

Another mistake is to go cheap. While being thrifty is a virtue, being cheap is wasteful because the item either will not do the job or will not last and have to be replaced soon. Cheap printers require expensive consumables. Cheap computers do not have the power to do the job. A cheap GPS will lack the accuracy needed for the project. Be thrifty, but do not be cheap.

Securing and maintaining data

The core of any GIS is data that covers the *who*, *what*, *when*, and *where*. Getting and maintaining data is easily the largest expense associated with a GIS.

Data acquisition

Consider how much information even the smallest community has. Much, if not most, GIS data comes from existing data, either inside or outside the organization. The building department, the public utilities, the planning department, the parks department, and the assessor's office all have data. Information stored in most existing databases, also known as legacy systems, is ripe for use in a GIS. When that data is combined with other data, it becomes a powerful source for new information. For example, connecting the permit system with the financial system in a local government can create a new way to process requests. CAD data, such as parcel maps and facility plans, can be converted fairly easily depending on the initial quality of the data. There may be other data on paper that can be scanned, such as substructure maps or plot plans of park facilities.

Scanning large amounts of material can be done in-house or through an outside firm with a fixed cost per page or per feature extracted. If there is a continuing stream of documents to scan, it makes sense to purchase a scanner to use in-house. With document imaging becoming a popular tool in government, scanners with document feeders for letter- and legal-sized paper are commonplace. If the scanning is more limited in nature, for example, converting old paper maps to gather historical data, then hiring an outside firm may be the better option. The discussion of scanners earlier in this chapter provides more detailed information on purchasing versus using a scanning service bureau.

Aerial photos are another useful source for data. Law enforcement personnel especially appreciate aerial photos. Having a photograph with parcel lines is very helpful in planning for event security, stakeouts, and apprehensions. Economic development staff often uses aerial photos for site marketing, especially in conjunction with site selection applications on the Internet. Orthophotography vendors contract with local firms specializing in taking the actual photos if they do not have their own planes, and the processing is completed at the vendor's facility. Such arrangements make it easy to locate a number of qualified vendors and get competitive pricing in any part of the country. The equipment involved in aerial photography is very expensive, so it generally cannot be done in-house. A digital photograph from the mayor's old biplane will not do.

The state and federal governments are also good sources for data. For example, the Census Bureau has created a GIS street network called the TIGER/Line® (Topologically Integrated Geographic Encoding and Referencing—a good Jeopardy!® question). While TIGER has address ranges, street names, and many other useful attributes, it is notoriously inaccurate. Streets can appear to be over one hundred feet off from their actual location. However, one intern for a town moved the TIGER streets to match the aerial photos in just a few days, creating sufficiently spatially accurate lines with good attributes and at a cost of only a few hundred dollars in staff time. Many federal data sources are available for free downloaded from the Geospatial One-Stop program online. While homeland security concerns have limited the availability of some data on the Internet, there is still much useful data for a community's GIS.

Buying datasets is another option. The cost of geographic data has dropped dramatically with much available for download from the Internet from sources like the Geography Network℠ *(www.geographynetwork.com)*. Commercial services offer information like street networks, packaged census data, environmentally

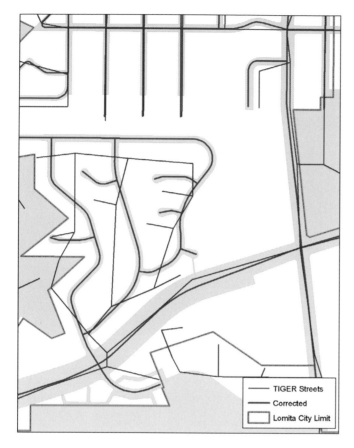

Figure 3.2 TIGER/Line data from the U.S. Census Bureau provides basic street networks for a GIS. When verified with data from aerial photography, it becomes an important data layer.

Source: Michael McDaniel, City of Lomita GIS

sensitive sites, and even satellite photos. On any purchased data, beware of licensing restrictions that may keep the data from being used the way it is needed. Worse yet, some licenses stipulate that any new data created using the licensed data belongs to the vendor. While that may not seem like a problem initially, it will become an issue when someone else needs to use the created information and they cannot have it without the vendor's permission or if the vendor requires the agency to stop using the data after the license expires.

Types of data

Different types of data within a GIS are often referred to as layers. The GIS uses these data layers, placing one on top of another and relating them to each other, to do a spatial analysis. One class of data is important enough for local governments to merit a separate discussion. Parcels are the core of most communities' GIS programs. Parcels represent tracts or plots of land. For example, they might denote the legal ownership for a piece of property or a designated land use within a city plan (Kennedy 2001). In an electronic format, they are referred to as digital parcels. Oftentimes another level of government may already have converted paper maps or computer-aided design (CAD) files into digital parcels that are ready to use in a GIS. Paper maps can be scanned or, using a program like ArcGIS® Survey Analyst,[1] precise lines can be created from legal descriptions to produce digital parcels. In any case, improved technology has greatly simplified creating digital parcels.

For data not tied to specific parcels or addresses, GPS is a handy tool. A GPS can pinpoint a given ground location based on longitude, latitude, and time measurements. Aerial photography is another tool that has become much less expensive. Using fixed survey points on the ground together with a GPS on the airplane, these photos can be made to overlay correctly with other mapped data.[2] Color photos where each pixel represents only three inches on the ground are becoming common. At that level of clarity, a hydrant is identifiable. Using interns working for two weeks, one city used existing aerial photos to map out 9.4 million square feet of sidewalks for the city's required asset inventory.

Some information simply does not exist, or mapping the existing data may show that it is not correct and needs to be redone. Infrastructure items like signs, street trees, water meters, manhole covers, traffic signals, and storm water catch basins do not have real addresses. Many other layers will have addresses, such as park program users, businesses, and crimes sites, but be out of date. Many types of data must be used in conjunction with other data, like bus routes which lie on top of streets, in order to be useful. Similarly, zoning is composed of parcels as are parks and schools layers.

Data limitations and restrictions

Accuracy is very important. While the immediate reaction may be to make all data perfectly accurate, it is not possible. In fact, it is important to define accurate means for each application. Can it be within five feet of its actual location, like street trees for tree maintenance purposes? Or does it have to be within one foot, like street trees for water system design purposes? Certainly, one layer of data can be used for many purposes, but only if it is accurate enough for each use. Using the tree example, data accurate to one foot could serve both needs. Data accurate to two feet would not. Noting the accuracy of each layer will help avoid such improper uses. The level of accuracy, collection date, and person who gathered the data are all examples of metadata, or information about the data that should be included in the layer.

Considering every likely use for a type of data will help determine the level of accuracy needed. The application requiring the highest precision determines what accuracy will be needed for that layer. With the tree layer described above, the water system requirement for one-foot precision would set the limit. Naturally, precision has a cost. At the highest end, a licensed surveyor will have to do the acquisition using specialized equipment. In practice, most GIS data is not survey grade and is not used for survey purposes. If the level of accuracy required for all the identified uses of the data makes the costs unaffordable, simply do not use the data for that purpose. The value of metadata is that anyone can see the accuracy of the data and determine its appropriate use.

Data maintenance

Most GIS layers need to be updated routinely. New streets are built, boundaries may change, parcels split or are merged, and traffic signals are added. Unless it is updated regularly with new data, the GIS will represent only a snapshot in time. At the same time, it is difficult to track changes. The answer is to create systems that automatically update themselves or at least create a notation when there has been a change. Many maintenance management systems now have such a link. When workers replace a sign, the database updates the GIS layer. There is no additional work for the field crews and no intervention required by the office staff to update it. Unfortunately, many older GIS systems as well as paper systems have no such capability. Considering how to keep each dataset regularly updated as part of the overall workflow can simplify the process.

Solutions to data problems

As soon as datasets are available, another agency will want them. A city will want a county's health permit data. A town will want a neighboring town's street data for doing more complete traffic studies. A water district will want a county's storm drain data. With the new focus on homeland security, state and national agencies want different types of data layers. Sharing data serves the taxpayers well. Occasionally, a formal data sharing agreement is used. More often, data sharing between agencies is a simple transaction between peers. Traffic engineers share traffic volumes, fire captains share evacuation routes, and planners share general plan data. The reason is simple: the overall value of the data to the public is higher if more agencies use it. All agencies can do a better job with better information.

Debate over data sales and licensing

Several years ago, staff in some communities promised elected officials and upper management that a GIS would pay for itself by creating data to sell. A membership survey by the Urban and Regional Information Systems Association (URISA) found that a significant number of the public agencies responding to the survey (85 percent) charge for GIS data and products (Croswell and Wernher 2004). And many city and county governments have adopted policies or mandates requiring their GIS programs recover costs through the sale of data and services. Certainly, it is not an uncommon practice.

That said, the ability to fully recover GIS expenses through data sales is nearly nonexistent. San Francisco, a very dense city with high levels of economic activity, was not able to make money selling data even when it dedicated staff to the effort. City officials could not even cover the costs of the sales effort. If a big city like San Francisco could not make such a business model work, it is unlikely to work in smaller communities. And the URISA survey notes that of the respondents who replied that have some form of fee schedule or pricing policy, only a handful (twenty-four agencies or about 12 percent) have generated significant revenue where fees for products are set at a level above the cost of distribution (Croswell and Wernher 2004).

There are other strong arguments against selling data. First, the most likely buyers are other public agencies, followed by the members of the general public. In either case, the taxpayers have already paid for the data collection and charging a fee would make them pay for it again, even though the data is in no way consumed by sharing it. Second, private use of GIS data is generally for economic development purposes. Unless communities do not want good jobs and quality development, they should disseminate their data. Third, a democracy requires free access to information, including geographic information, used as a decision-making tool.

Finally, some local government GIS professionals argue they worked hard creating datasets and should not be forced to give it away to private concerns for commercial purposes. However, it is not their data, and they were already paid by the public agency. Even when data is given to a private company, it is still going to support local needs. A tourist who buys a map created with free public data uses that map to spend money in town. As will be discussed later in this chapter, there are much better ways to pay for GIS than selling data.

Some organizations attach licensing restrictions to their data. In no way is there agreement on the subject. Some GIS professionals feel it is absolutely necessary while others feel it should never be done by a public agency. Licensing puts limits on who can have access to the data and how the data can be used. Some require registration and a statement describing how the data will be used before releasing it, although most states do not allow such restrictions. The major concern is that without licensing, the data will be used for a purpose other than that for which it was intended, especially that it will be used for a purpose that surpasses the data's accuracy. Being out of date is another concern, as is a fear that errors in the data may create a situation of liability. On this final issue, there is no evidence of any community being successfully sued because someone used that community's erroneous data. Recently, a new type of license simply states the user must recognize the limitations of the data and give credit to the creating agency. Most agencies do not require licenses on their data. To do so is a local decision to the extent permitted by law.

In some states, GIS data is a public record that cannot be sold for more than the cost of providing it, and there can be no restrictions on its use. In those states, that is simply the end of the discussion, although some agencies have tried to ignore the law until forced to do otherwise. It is best to check state laws to find out if geographic data is considered a public record and if there are restrictions on licensing or selling data. During the start-up phase of a GIS, agency attorneys will likely not be knowledgeable on the subject. Check with local GIS user group members to get the latest rules since their attorneys will likely have already done the research.

Confidential data

Clearly, not all information should be made public. Privacy and safety concerns keep some data confidential. Internet-based property information systems in some cities make it easy to find who owns a particular piece of property, but they do not allow a search by owner name to find where someone lives. Names and addresses of crime victims are confidential. Business information, such as gross sales, may be confidential. The public need for information must be weighed against the privacy concerns of the individual. One solution is to generalize data, for example, showing criminal activity by block or larger area instead of a specific address.

Safety concerns must also be balanced against the public's needs. In the aftermath of September 11, many agencies pulled geographic data off the Internet for fear that it would aid terrorists in planning attacks. Some went as far as removing information that was available in the phone book. In response to these concerns, the Federal Geographic Data Committee (FGDC) developed guidelines to help determine what information should be public and how it should be disseminated. The guidelines are written in plain English and include an easy-to-follow decision tree to consider the usefulness of certain data for planning an attack, data availability from other sources, and whether security risks outweigh the societal benefits of disseminating the data. The guidelines are available on the FGDC Web site *(www.fgdc.gov)*.

Table 3.1   FGDC framework for analyzing the homeland security sensitivity of geospatial data and information sources

Filter key questions for decision makers	
Usefulness	• Is the information useful for target selection or location purposes? • Is the information useful for attack planning purposes?
Uniqueness	• Is the information readily available from other geospatial information sources? • Is the information available from direct observation or other nongeospatial information types?
Societal benefits and costs	• What are the expected security benefits of restricting public access to the source? • What are the expected societal costs of restricting public access to the source?

Source: Baker et al. 2004

Table 3.2   Troubleshooting problems with a GIS

Problem	Reason for the problem	Example of the problem	Solution	Benefits of the solution
No plan	Manager gets excited, buys equipment with no idea of what to do with it	Spend the budget on a scanner instead of training, or vice versa	Make at least a basic outline and make sure everyone knows what it is	A smoother implementation and better use of scarce resources
Too much plan, no action	A fear of doing something wrong leads to endless study and planning	So much effort goes into planning out each detail that nothing ever happens	Recognize it is impossible and unnecessary to know and plan for every detail	A plan that gets implemented and updated over time
Lack of management support	Management does not see how GIS will help them	GIS seems focused narrowly or is identified as just another piece of expensive technology	Show how GIS addresses problems important to management	GIS becomes a part of addressing the community's issues
Lack of IT infrastructure	Organization is very small or has operated with manual systems	Limited NoData network or technology support	Since GIS is much more useful as an enterprise system, use this as an opportunity to create information technology infrastructure	An enterprise-wide GIS supports more than one area and connects the work of multiple departments
Unrealistic expectations	Failure to clearly explain what is to happen	Users believe they will all get their priorities met at the same time	Lay out an implementation schedule that gives a general idea of when each need will be addressed	Users are more likely to support a plan they believe to be realistic, even if it does not place their projects first
Copying someone else	It looks easier to do what worked somewhere else rather than develop a local plan	Implementation focuses on the water department first, although the public works department has far more data already	Use another town's success to generate ideas and solutions	Learn from others' successes and failures while not being locked into their processes or priorities

Source: Reprinted with permission from John C. Baker et al. Mapping the Risks: Assessing the Homeland Security Implications of Publicly Available Geospatial Information. MG 142-NGA, Santa Monica, Calif.: Rand Corporation, 2004. Rand©

Staffing

A vital part of any system is the people. Be they full-time staff, contractors, or employees who do GIS as one aspect of their job, they are the ones who will make the system a useful service. While contractors are not generally responsible for the entire GIS, there are some organizations that choose to contract out the service to gain increased flexibility and access to high skill levels. The contractor takes care of recruiting, administrative responsibilities, training, and other management functions with oversight by the organization. This is more often found in organizations that already contract for general information technology services and is generally contracted with the same company.

A more common approach is to use contractors for limited-term projects or specific ongoing services. A consultant may gather the data and conduct an analysis for a proposed development when the county does not have the expertise on staff or does not have the staff time available for the project. Commonly, communities contract for labor-intensive, but short-term, projects like citywide GPS data gathering. Local staff then maintains the data. Some projects may require technical expertise, such as programming skills, that is not needed often enough to justify a full-time staff member in a smaller organization. The contractor may maintain certain applications from the company's offices or do the work on site.

When considering contracting, use the guidelines described earlier in the discussion of developing a GIS plan. There are enough qualified firms to create a healthy competition to get the best quality and price possible for the service desired. Being a tough negotiator and looking out for the community's interests is not the same thing as being unpleasant and unreasonable. Organizations with bad reputations may find they get few responses to a request for proposals. Treat them fairly, provide a reasonable work space if needed, and pay them on time to make them a partner in the success of the GIS. A well-established reputation for being a good partner will make it much easier to find other firms with which to do projects.

Assigning GIS responsibilities

Will GIS staff consist of people who are already in the organization or new employees? New employees bring technical knowledge and experience with other ways to do business, but existing employees have knowledge of the organization that is useful beyond technical skills. One area to look for existing employees is in occupations that are otherwise becoming obsolete, such as drafting technicians who do intensive manual work. Most of these people will be open to retraining, although it can be difficult emotionally for some of them to go through a change. Supportive management with a positive attitude can make the difference for them. There will also be staff members who see their role evolve, such as a planner who does some GIS gradually shifting to be a GIS person who does some planning and eventually assuming the role of GIS support. The same is often true for engineers and management analysts.

In a smaller community, all the GIS staff may have primary job responsibilities in other areas. Since GIS is an add-on to the employee's existing duties, management must be sure there is enough time to give each activity its due. Assuming someone can always do one more thing is the road to a frustrated employee doing a mediocre job on each task. Clear at least some other work responsibilities off the staff member's plate in order to allow her to give proper attention to the GIS. This is especially true if the employee managing the GIS operation also has other responsibilities.

When a community is getting started in GIS, the manager will often come from within the organization. Knowledge of the organization can be more important than knowledge of GIS in the beginning. And some current employees may apply for GIS positions. They should be considered based on their existing knowledge and ability to be trained for the position. The key is in having a team of people who, between them, have knowledge of both the organization and GIS. Train existing staff on technical matters and new staff on how the organization operates. GIS is a tool, and the staff must understand existing operations of the organization to use the tool to its fullest.

Before long the demand for services will likely justify a full-time GIS staff, even if it is only one position that has other technical duties assigned to it. For a larger operation, a number of people may be needed to support the many departments. To get sample job descriptions, check with members of the local GIS user group. The Urban and Regional Information Systems Association (URISA) puts out a publication with up-to-date descriptions for GIS jobs at all levels in organizations large and small. URISA also conducts a national salary survey that can serve as a general guide. Beware that salaries vary greatly by region. Check with other local governments to be competitive in compensation. Compare with other organizations of a similar size if possible. Another way to set pay rates is to compare GIS positions with other positions in the organization based on level of responsibility, experience required, and job duties.

There are many sources for recruiting qualified staff. Local user groups are a great place to announce job openings. If they have an e-mail list or Web site, those would reach a good pool of qualified local talent. Universities and colleges can recommend recent graduates or alumni who are interested in a change. These options are very low or no cost. National job boards for GIS positions are well publicized. While costs for these services vary, they are generally less than the cost of a newspaper ad. Ask GIS personnel from other jurisdictions to assist in the selection process. They can review applicants' technical qualifications to determine if they are up-to-date and can meet the organization's needs.

Interns are a valuable addition to any community's GIS. They are inexpensive and bring an excitement to their work. Colleges and universities are an obvious place to look for interns. Many communities have an ongoing relationship with a local educational institution, serving as a training place for students and a testing ground for new technologies. Some communities use older high school students on special projects. In fact, there have been some real successes in that area, encouraging promising students to pursue careers in GIS and government in general. Interns often develop into permanent full-time staff. Working with faculty helps the local government remain an active part of the campus GIS program. A drawback of interns is the high turnover and need to train each new intern. Interns, without any permanent GIS staff, are not a long-term solution.

GIS data collection and staffing in Manhattan Beach, California

Data collection and maintenance is one of the most demanding elements of managing a GIS. The City of Manhattan Beach has taken an innovative approach to staffing GIS data collection and maintenance through its GIS/Public Works Light-Duty Alternative Work Program.

The program started when several employees from the public works department were injured on the job. Rather than being forced to stay home and collect disability pay (at two-thirds of their regular salary), workers can opt to participate in the program. These light-duty employees are reassigned to the city's GIS division where they collect and verify data. These employees' working knowledge of the city's infrastructure adds considerable value to the data collection effort. They know what infrastructure features look like, such as electrical control meters and backflow devices, and frequently bring back additional information about the features.

Since the program began in 1999, ten light-duty employees have taken advantage of this option. They worked for the GIS division for anywhere from a few days to several months. The results so benefited all involved that the program has been expanded. During downtimes, such as rainy days, regular-duty employees can also be assigned to participate in the program. Some employees have had GIS data collection duties added to their job responsibilities as a result of their participation in the program.

Based on materials provided by Bonnie Shrewsbury, GIS analyst with the City of Manhattan Beach, Calif.

Training

From bringing new skills to the organization or keeping skills current, training cannot be neglected. One city councilman said that training was not the city's responsibility. "Employees should know what they need to know when they start here," he said. Luckily for the city, his fellow council members did not agree. The world is not static. There are new demands and new ways to deal with old problems. Any technology field like GIS requires training to get the most out of the city's investment.

If enough people need to be trained, many vendors will offer training on site, saving the cost of travel and reducing the cost of the class itself. Some communities share training programs to lower costs. There may be qualified staff in one community that can train others. In Los Angeles, a regional council of governments had staff members from two cities conduct classes at a third city's training facility. People from eight agencies attended the training at a much lower cost than if they had sent people to a regular class. The instructors were given a bonus by the other cities in addition to their regular pay. The response was so good that they immediately had more people ask to sign up for a second class, creating an ongoing program. A side benefit was the students formed a community of support that lasted beyond the class itself.

By sending employees to formal training offsite, they are free of the disruptions of the office and can better concentrate. Many software companies offer training at sites around the country. Colleges and universities provide training on specific software and regular classes on the concepts involved. Many of them offer certificate programs aimed at various aspects of the field. Each has its own focus, allowing the consumer to select a program based on his needs. If there are several programs in the area, consider and evaluate each of them to determine the best fit.

Local or regional user groups are a useful part of any training program. They are a venue to share ideas and problems. Most have presentations by vendors promoting new ideas and members showing their projects. In addition, they are an opportunity to meet other GIS practitioners who can serve as advisors to help with difficult problems or just exchange ideas on shared problems. Attending user group meetings is well worth the time it takes away from the work place.

Like user group meetings, conferences provide an opportunity to see new ideas and meet other practitioners. While some organizations may see conferences as a frill or special perk, there is no other activity that packs as much content into a short span of time as a good conference. There are regional and national conferences, some put together by vendors like ESRI and others by user associations like URISA. Many offer scholarships or student assistantships for those financially unable to attend otherwise.

Especially for isolated communities, off-site training is a difficult option, and there may not be any training vendors in the area. ESRI® Virtual Campus provides many courses in GIS technology and specific software via the Internet. Some universities offer distance learning for their programs. If the best program is across the country, that may not be a barrier to participating. There are also tutorials and books available with in-depth material. Even communities in or near major metropolitan areas find these options helpful in their GIS training.

Besides the core GIS users, there will be casual users and individuals who use only a specific application. Especially at the beginning of a GIS program, there should be general training for staff members to understand how they can use GIS even if that means just knowing what to ask for from GIS staff. This kind of training might be viewed as an orientation instead of training. If the organization does some sort of annual GIS Day event as described earlier, it can address this need.

For end users, like planners or crime analysts who are assisted by GIS in their daily work, training can keep people excited about their jobs. A new way to attack a problem creates enthusiasm. The training can be outside the office or done through other staff. The primary purpose is to help people do their jobs and not just add an additional task to their day. Applications need to be usable and data securely maintained, or staff will lose confidence in them and perhaps quietly go back to the old manual systems they feel they can count on.

GIS training in Kissimmee, Florida

The City of Kissimmee places considerable emphasis on staff training. The practice stems from the belief that the more employees know and can work through issues independently, the more tasks and projects they can complete with minimal assistance from the information technology (IT) department. With a GIS team of three supporting some five hundred users throughout the city government, it is primarily a question of efficiency and how to best use available staff time.

Staff learns about GIS applications via custom in-house training and Web training provided through the IT department. During the training, GIS staff encourages users to suggest future functions for applications. Most general GIS users are taught in-house through the IT department. Department GIS leaders and GIS staff themselves are trained by ESRI certified trainers or take courses from ESRI's Virtual Campus.

Matthew Cieri, a GIS specialist with the City of Kissimmee, encourages staff self-training through a variety of available resources. "The GIS community is probably the best group for sharing information. Everyone seems to be willing to help one way or another," he said. Cieri points to program documentation, listservs, user forums, and online help as important options for saving time and energy. For example, programming questions submitted to a user forum will yield, within hours, code samples or other suggestions to make a particular task easier. An electronic knowledge base for common issues prevents GIS staff from wasting time developing a fix that already exists.

Cieri also recommends tapping into other resources, such as developer samples, available online and on CD. Third-party applications, especially those from an established company, can greatly increase the functionality of a GIS application. They cost a few hundred dollars but save staff time and increase productivity. In short, Kissimmee sees training as a worthwhile investment, saving both time and money for the city in the long run.

Based on "Local government: Small staff, lots of work; what to do?" a paper by Matthew Cieri presented at the 2004 ESRI International User Conference, August 9-13, 2004 in San Diego, Calif.

Web-based applications require the least amount of training because most people feel comfortable using the Internet. Well-designed applications are clear and easy to use. One agency developed an application that allowed people in many agencies to enter data into it. Each agency had a one-hour training session scheduled. None of them took more than a few minutes for their training, and none needed a follow-up visit. Some of them were even trained over the phone.

Organizational structure

Where should the GIS be located in the organizational structure? Where is not as important as recognizing the potential impact of the decision. Knowing the benefits and drawbacks allows for measures to limit the drawbacks. The first choice is between a centralized and a decentralized operation. A central GIS division ensures better coordination of activities. There is little duplication of effort. Sharing information between different users is simple. A decentralized structure, with GIS work being done in various departments, ensures the GIS efforts go directly to support the work of the operating departments. Active users and data creators are in each work area.

Another option is to house GIS in one department that has active and supportive users. The person who championed GIS will most likely be a part of that department. While there will be difficulties serving users outside that department, serving other departments' GIS needs will likely foster cooperation in other areas. For example, often a GIS will start in a utility such as a water department. Communication between utility departments and other departments is usually very limited. But with additional effort and encouragement from upper management, the water department can consider the GIS needs of economic development staff. Improved communication among diverse departments is a great benefit.

Early GIS required specialized and expensive equipment and software, and usually had to be contained in one area. Most current desktop computers can run the software, and a GIS can be used anywhere staff is. With applications running on the Internet, GIS is extended to users outside the organization, including the public. Most communities are moving to a mix of centralized and decentralized operations. There may be a small core staff in information services or attached to the city or county manager's office. They will provide support to departments, maintain basic layers of information and Internet applications, and manage centralized databases. Departments will have their own GIS users handling projects and data for their needs. There may be regular meetings to coordinate projects and discuss matters of mutual concern.

In a large city, there may be a GIS department with many full-time users. In a small city with thirty employees, there may be one person who handles most GIS needs among other job responsibilities. Structure depends on the size of the community and how its government operations are organized. However, the structure does not have to dictate the funding. There can be a centralized department with many departments providing some funds, either for staffing or perhaps just ink and paper. A decentralized operation can still have funds all budgeted in one area. While it does not show a detailed breakdown of costs by project, it is very simple and shows the total cost of GIS.

Larger organizations often have formal cross charging for services like GIS provided by one department to another. Cross charging better shows the true cost of an activity and encourages departments wanting a particular service to support funding for it. There are also drawbacks to that approach. Not all GIS activities are easily contained in any one department. In fact, most GIS work benefits multiple departments. Was the

Organizing for GIS in Anaheim, California

Anaheim is one of the fastest growing cities in California and the country. Managing such phenomenal growth requires a robust system that can analyze voluminous amounts of information. In 1997, the Anaheim City Council invested in an enterprise GIS to better maintain and manage geographic information. The first step in building the new system was for staff to convert the city's CAD (computer-assisted design) basemaps to a GIS format.

As more and more layers of data were developed, GIS users became frustrated with accessing the files over the network. The layers were stored on a central file server and, due to their large size, took a fair amount of time to download. Oftentimes, employees would opt to copy the files to the hard drives of their desktop computers to increase performance. This led to the multiple copies of data layers in the system. Sometimes the data was current, sometimes it was not. There was no metadata to define when a new layer was created and what data was used. The reliability of the GIS system was in question.

To eliminate the redundant copies of data being accessed by the city's GIS users, the public utilities department volunteered to support the core functions of the overall GIS program. These functions included (1) administering GIS software and databases, (2) maintaining the base layers such as parcels and streets, and (3) developing applications for citywide use. This core GIS group provides some support to other city departments, but the departments use their own staff to build and maintain data and applications specific to their needs.

This approach combines that of a centralized model (the core GIS support staff) with a decentralized model (GIS staff located within each department). The result is that each department can set its own pace to develop GIS data and applications based on its needs and budget constraints. At the same time, Anaheim's enterprise GIS is ensured of having base data layers that are up-to-date and accurate. The city's various departments benefit from each other's work and need not compete for services from a large centralized GIS unit. The primary beneficiaries are the customers and residents of Anaheim who have access to the greatest depth of data and information available.

Based on materials provided by Mark Lopez

traffic volume data for the traffic engineer or the economic development staff? Both departments will want the other to pay.

And how do overhead costs get distributed? In one organization, cross charging became a fine art, with one employee assigned in nearly every department to find ways to charge other departments and generate revenue. The result was higher costs and unhealthy competition instead of cooperation to address the organization's overall goals. Cross charging requires oversight from top management to maintain the focus on a common purpose. Structure can change as the GIS develops over time. Centralized or decentralized staffing or budgeting can work as long as management recognizes the costs and benefits from the start and makes all users of the system stakeholders in its success.

What are the mistakes to avoid in staffing and organization? Most importantly, don't assume a GIS is ever complete. The world changes and the GIS must change too. Training must continue or staff knowledge will become stale. Using old job specifications will help only in hiring people with out-of-date skills. Pay rates cannot be based on another part of the country or national averages. Compensation alone will not keep good employees. Do not rely on one person to do everything. One day that person will leave, and the GIS will effectively be gone as well. How GIS is organized is not as important as that it be focused on the community's goals. A successful GIS will involve people throughout the organization as partners serving the public.

Paying for GIS

Far too many people in local government think GIS is expensive. They have heard stories about local governments spending hundreds of thousand of dollars in the early 1990s to get going. But prices for hardware have dropped radically, and with the advent of the Internet, there is less software needed to serve GIS to the entire enterprise. Perhaps the first rule of budgeting should be to ignore what people in the next county spent, even if it was only five years ago. Unless the plan is to do significantly more than that county did, the cost will likely be less. Is it then best to wait five more years? No, because GIS is already affordable, and the community is missing out on many benefits that far outweigh the cost.

Earlier sections in this chapter discussed the costs of GIS: staffing, hardware, software, and data. Some of these are one time expenses, like the creation of parcel data. Others are occasional expenses, like replacing hardware every few years or getting new aerial photos. Others are ongoing, particularly staffing, data updates, and supplies. Considering all of these in budgeting creates reasonable expectations for what can or cannot be accomplished and makes a successful GIS more certain. The in-depth case study accompanying this chapter discusses how Gunnison County in rural Colorado relied on innovative funding and careful planning to establish its successful GIS program.

Cost savings and reduced expenses

Where does money come from for GIS? First, take a look at some ideas that deserve questioning. Cost savings is an abused area in technology projects. How often is the claim made that a GIS project will reduce staff? Some GIS applications do reduce the need for staff, but it is often redirected to other areas. For example, many drafting technicians become GIS workers, so the organization gets more productivity from them, but there is no reduction in total expenditures. Still, there may be significant savings. Examine what it costs to perform an activity without GIS and what it would cost using GIS. If GIS can cut the time taken for the process from two weeks to two days, there is a value of that to the organization and to the public. More often, GIS allows an activity to be done in-house at a low cost, avoiding what was previously a cost paid to a third party. GIS can also take care of the small tasks, allowing staff to concentrate on the more important issues.

Look at the long-term value of decisions. Typically, selecting a site for a public facility has relied heavily on the instincts and experience of staff. The process can be very time consuming and subject to second guessing by elected officials and the public. Using GIS for site selection gets a quick answer to spatial questions. For a fire station, those questions would include average and maximum call times for each location, location of vacant parcels of a certain size, location of hazardous material handlers, and distance to certain critical facilities. It is easy to create multiple scenarios using different criteria.

After an addition to a middle school had started construction in Massachusetts, a group of high school students in the community undertook a GIS project to calculate attendance areas. They weighed all the factors and came up with areas that met all the district guidelines while keeping students in the same schools as their neighbors. They presented their findings to the school board. The district's hired consultant had not used GIS and had not created a solution anywhere near as mutually agreeable. He sat quietly and uncomfortably as the students showed how GIS could come up with a better solution more quickly and cheaply than a consultant who had made many such plans over the years.

Avoiding costs can be a huge savings area. Imagine being sued less often by citizens who tripped on sidewalks. In the city of Manhattan Beach, California, an inventory of sidewalk problem areas overlaid with tree types by street showed a clear correlation, leading to the creation of a new maintenance schedule based on tree species. The result was reductions in accidents and punitive damages assessed because the courts could see the city was making a clear effort to address the problem. Likewise, accurate water system maps combined with an inventory of easements can pinpoint missing easements, which helped one city avoid the cost of relocating a water main.

One area of infrastructure maintenance lends itself particularly well to GIS. Pavement management protects most communities' most expensive assets—their streets. Proper maintenance can extend the life of a street considerably and reduce maintenance costs. GIS can strengthen a pavement management program, helping to cluster projects, consider related streets, and show decision makers the impact of deferred maintenance. It is much easier to visualize current and projected conditions on a map than in a tabular format.

Just as selling data is generally not considered a big money maker, selling maps will not likely generate much cash. Map production can be very time consuming, and some states do not allow local agencies to sell maps for more than the cost of production. Most maps will be produced for community groups that object to paying or businesses that generate taxes far in excess of the cost of a few maps.

While a map may not cost much, the economic activity it can generate is worth huge amounts of property, business, and sales taxes, in addition to the new jobs brought to the community. The value of data is not in selling it, but in using it. One Los Angeles–area community found helping locate a new fast food restaurant brought in about $15,000 annually in sales tax in addition to other taxes. If using GIS helps locate just one desired business, it can create a long-term revenue stream for the community. GIS is extremely valuable as an economic development tool. In fact, economic development is a growing GIS focus for many communities. One important strategy for economic development in many states is redevelopment of blighted areas, including business attraction and retention, land assembly, infrastructure improvements, brownfields reuse, and development subsidy. GIS provides many analysis and marketing tools, making the redevelopment agency the leading source of GIS funding in communities with an active redevelopment program or at least a significant contributor.

Government Accounting Standards Board (GASB) Statement No. 34 requires each community to develop an inventory of all its infrastructure assets to ensure long-term maintenance. Failure to comply can reduce a city's bond rating, raising the cost of issuing bonds or borrowing funds. Communities using GIS to comply with GASB 34 requirements have found that in addition to complying with the regulations, they have useful data for infrastructure maintenance and planning. Communities not using GIS often have no useful by-products from their GASB 34 efforts.

Begin to identify any of these potential savings or avoided expenses, and revenue increases to the maximum extent possible. When budget discussions come, it will not be hard to show GIS has paid for itself well in excess of what could have been done selling data and without the administrative burden of sales.

Grants are very popular and helpful in the public sector, but they rarely can be used for exactly what the community wants and they often come with serious strings attached. Even more rarely will they fund continuing operations. Look for vendor grants that provide hardware, software, or data to do something important in the community. Participating in local user groups can be a good source of information about the existence of grants from various sources. Flexibility in seeing how a grant can be adapted to a local problem helps get the most out of a grant.

Collecting missed revenues is another way for GIS to pay for itself. By overlaying water meter records with business licenses, staff in one city identified businesses that did not have licenses. This meant that sales taxes were not going to the city in addition to missing the business license revenue. Geographic analysis can identify sales taxes going to the wrong jurisdiction. GIS-based property assessment ensures property owners pay their fair share. Appraisals are done more quickly, more accurately, and more fairly, thus reducing the number of appeals.

Nonmonetary benefits

Consider also the important nonmonetary benefits of GIS. These often far outweigh the monetary benefits. Better traffic planning or crime analysis can actually save lives. What is it worth to a city council member not to have to attend the funeral of a child killed in an accident on a city street when it could have been prevented by a GIS analysis of traffic accident data? Fire run maps cut the time it takes response crews to reach an emergency and show the location of the nearest hydrant, again saving valuable seconds. While there are models for determining the economic value of almost anything, the noneconomic value can be far more important.

Funding strategies

Utilities are a common source of funding because GIS is so useful to them, from system planning to notifying customers of anticipated service interruptions. There are two types of utilities, those that have GIS and those that are going to get it. A municipal utility can use the data created for its needs to serve the GIS needs of the entire municipality, often making the water department the primary funding GIS source.

In any agency, look to the departments that have funds and see how GIS can serve them. It is unlikely that GIS could not help them address some significant issue. Since data created for one area serves the whole enterprise, one or two funding departments can often create a GIS that serves everyone's needs.

Sharing costs is an option where agencies share some or all of the same geographic area. A school district, flood control district, housing authority, and a health care district are examples of agencies that might share resources with each other and the local municipality with members being responsible for maintaining various layers of information. In some cases, one partner may simply provide GIS services for other agencies in exchange for direct funding. Beyond the efficiencies of such a system, there is an enormous benefit in increased interagency cooperation.

Many counties have discovered the value of cooperating with their cities and towns. In Ventura County, California, the county maintains parcel data and other layers for all the cities. Under the original system, the county attempted to sell the data at full cost, and none of the cities would or could afford to buy it. Under the new system, the county provides the data in exchange for a nominal contribution from each city. The county gets funds to help with data maintenance, and the cities get good quality data at a reasonable cost. Plus, the friction caused by the old system has been replaced by an atmosphere of cooperation and a shared purpose in providing service to the public.

Neighboring communities may find sharing costs with each other, and even sharing staff, serves their needs especially if they share the same school district or other special district. They may share more expensive equipment, such as a high-end GPS receiver, or an Internet application and the staff needed to maintain it. A consortium of smaller communities can even create a shared GIS operation, providing them services well beyond what they could afford individually. Again, the value of cooperation extends well beyond GIS.

As described earlier, local colleges and universities can be excellent partners, providing staff for field work and acting as a great resource for identifying and securing grants. They may offer training for staff at reduced rates.

Some vendors offer financing for larger purchases, allowing the user to spread payments over time as the benefits emerge. Leasing, bundled with maintenance, also enables an agency to lower the upfront costs of hardware purchases and avoid maintenance costs without having to deal with out-of-date equipment. Annual lease payments become fixed costs an agency can plan on. For some communities, these can be important considerations.

The Open Data Consortium Project (see sidebar on page 53) has put together a list of ten ways to support GIS, including several of the ideas described above. There are many ways to look at funding. Cost savings, cost sharing, improvements in efficiency, revenue enhancements, grants, and financing can all help toward paying for GIS, usually in combination. There is no single formula for success. There are many avenues that can work for any community. GIS has enough value to any organization that it is not difficult to decide to move forward. Deciding how to fund it should not be difficult either. Every day, a GIS will provide a valuable service that matters in how people do their work. There is no reason to be shy about the contribution that GIS is making. With a little encouragement, people from throughout the organization can be important allies to ensure stable funding.

Creative financing ideas for funding a local government GIS

The Open Data Consortium Project *(www.opendataconsortium.org)* was organized by Bruce Joffe, an Oakland-based GIS consultant, in collaboration with GeoData Alliance, a nonprofit coalition of geographic interests, and URISA, the international association of GIS professionals. The project focuses on developing a model policy for distributing governmental geospatial data. Research done by the consortium has uncovered ten key ways to support a local government GIS.

1. Capture increased revenues that come from greater economic activity and new economic development.
Undeveloped or underdeveloped sites provide little or no revenue for a local government. Helping business find appropriate sites through a GIS application can bring in new revenues by expanding the tax base, not increasing tax rates. Capturing those increased revenues or a portion of them helps ensure the GIS program continued success.

2. Secure increased revenues stemming from more accurate determination of facility locations for taxation purposes.
Using GIS capabilities can help more accurately locate undertaxed, taxable entities within different tax rate areas. Known as geoauditing, this process can identify more exact locations to secure increased revenues. Examples of such revenue sources include telephone franchises for E-911 (enhanced 911, which provides dispatchers with the location and phone number of callers), electricity and gas franchise fees, homestead exemptions, point-of-sale sales tax, personal and business property tax, and many other types of revenue sources.

3. Recover revenue produced from specific taxes and fees.
Land records maintenance and management are a major responsibility for local governments. Allocating a portion of the property transfer fee to support a GIS program, for instance, is an investment that significantly improves a jurisdiction's ability to do this task effectively.

4. Allocate a portion of funding for specific programs.
Many local government departments have independently funded programs that benefit from GIS, and could help recover the cost of a GIS program. For example, the analysis necessary to operate an ongoing sewer maintenance program requires building and maintaining a GIS basemap.

5. Charge fees for customer-specific online applications.
Common examples are recreational maps for residents or visitors and building permit programs. Local engineering and survey firms may also want to subscribe to a local government GIS in order to have direct access to digital data.

6. Charge fees for geoprocessing management services to other agencies.
For advanced GIS programs with the capacity, management services can be offered for a fee to other nearby jurisdictions or other entities. Offering such services saves time, money, and effort for the jurisdictions using the service and support for the GIS program providing the service.

7. Account for cost savings from geospatial analysis of public services programs.
Many cities have used their GIS to conduct geospatial analyses that resulted in significant cost savings. For example, an analysis of response times for fire protection services can reduce facility needs, thereby saving the locality on infrastructure investments.

8. Account for cost savings from coordinated management of public works infrastructure.
Preventing multiple digs for street maintenance projects or installing fiber-optic lines results in considerable cost savings. A portion of the savings should be reallocated to maintain the agency's geodata.

Creative financing ideas for funding a local government GIS (cont.)

9. Allocate a portion of each department's operating budget to support GIS services.
If a centralized model is used for a local government GIS, then all local government departments stand to benefit from the service. In such instances, it makes sense that a portion of the departments' operating budgets be devoted toward paying for benefits GIS affords them.

10. Allocate a portion of the general fund for enterprise-wide GIS operations.
To ensure fair and equitable access to a centralized GIS, top management can fund a local government GIS program directly. Doing so ensures that the responsibility for funding GIS is shared by all.

Based on "Ten ways to support GIS without selling data," by Bruce Joffe, October, 2003, from the Open Data Consortium Project Web site.

Avoiding mistakes

A final few thoughts about potential mistakes to avoid:

- Do not expect to make money selling data or services. Do make money by creating value for the organization and the community as a whole.
- Do not use the same funding method as the next town. Do recognize local differences that may make some sources more appropriate for the community than others.
- Do not buy hardware and software if the organization is not ready to use them. Do purchase items when they are needed.
- Do not expect to get continuing funding without showing value for the expense. Do show decision makers and the entire organization what GIS is doing to make government operations more effective and efficient.

Profile—County government	
Location	West Central Colorado
Size (miles square)	3,259 square miles
Population	13,956 (2000)
Form of government	County commission/administrator
Annual GIS operating budget	$150,000
Number of employees in GIS unit	2.5 FTE's
Governmental departments using GIS	9

Overview

Located in western Colorado, Gunnison County is a geographically large rural county. Despite limited resources for a GIS program, the county has built a robust system through solid planning and an innovative approach to funding.

Background

In the early 1990s, officials in Gunnison County began to discuss the need for a computer system to coordinate information within the county. The county's assessor and clerk, in particular, advocated a system that would allow their offices to access information from multiple sources in an automated fashion. In 1996, the county commissioners assigned the new county administrator the task of developing a highly sophisticated computer system that would include a GIS.

In 1998, the county's initial GIS application was a parcel mapping program. Parcel maps delineate land boundaries, including the dimensions and identification number of a lot. A parcel mapping program takes that information and records it in the GIS in a digital format that makes it easy to call up. Such programs are particularly useful for planning and land-use analysis purposes.

The county decided to use an outside contractor to build the data layer for the system but ran into problems when it discovered that the firm had not taken into consideration the number of mining claims in the county.[1] It became a struggle to finish the initial data layer. As a result, what was originally envisioned as an eighteen-month process took three years to complete.

The county's chief executive officer, John DeVore, managed expectations during this start-up phase of the GIS. He took a two-pronged approach to the situation. First, he kept all the stakeholders in the system informed about its progress, including problems they were experiencing. Second, he held the contractor's proverbial "feet to the fire," reminding principals in the firm that they should have been familiar with the nuances of the area prior to submitting a bid. "We had [the contractor] focus on the areas that were easiest to put together, and then move to the areas that were hardest to do," said DeVore.

As a result of the delays during start-up, the county's return on investment took some time to kick in but the system has proven its worth. "What I've seen is the ability for the staff to manage an incredible amount of additional projects and workload without an increase in FTEs," said De Vore. Housing authority tasks that once required help from the private sector, such as land banking and looking for parcels, is done in-house. "We don't have to do the dog work anymore; it's just a matter of point, click, and drag," he said.

The county's GIS use has evolved. According to Dave Michaelson, director of long-range planning and GIS for Gunnison County, the system began as a parcel-level database, but has grown to be an important analytic tool for the county. "We can use it to help the commissioners make better land-use decisions. We used it extensively in the comprehensive plan process. . .. We have as many environmental attributes as any place I have ever worked. The only way to manage that sort of information is within a GIS that's pretty robust," Michaelson said.

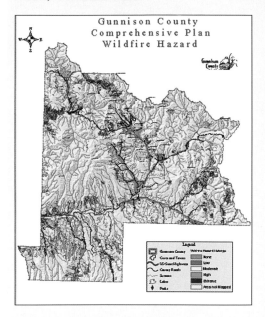

Figure 3.3 The rich diversity of Gunnison County's environmental attributes made initial data collection an enormous task. Having that data in digital form has enabled the county to develop some very innovative maps, such as this one showing potential wildfire areas.

Source: Gunnison County, Colo.

The county has used its GIS primarily for internal purposes, but expects to make the GIS data available to the public via the Internet. Michaelson observed, "There will be disclaimers associated with the data when appropriate. We've still got some work to do, but I think it's a really exciting step for us."

Needs assessment and setting priorities

The county uses a combination of formal and informal methods to assess needs and set priorities for building out its GIS. For example, the county underwent a major update of its comprehensive plan in 2004. In doing so, the county surveyed residents about what attributes in the local landscape were important to them. In addition to this survey data, the county also regularly tracks the number and type of requests it receives to determine what information the public wants. These two sources of information help determine what type of mapping work is needed by the broader community.

In addition to collecting data from the public, the county used eight special focus groups to prepare proposed language for each section of the comprehensive plan. These groups required a variety of information from the county's GIS department to complete their assigned tasks. Jim Starr, a commissioner for Gunnison County, pointed out that the work of the GIS is very much program-driven as opposed to information-driven. "We really try to tie it into the needs we have for the various programs," he said.

Given the small size of its GIS department, the county frequently must use a "fire drill management" approach—simply responding to needs as they come in—more than they would like, Michaelson admitted.

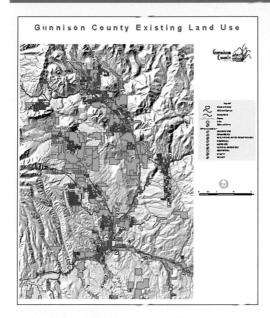

Figure 3.4 Land-use maps, such as this one, help Gunnison County commissioners develop the county's comprehensive plan.

Source: Gunnison County, Colo.

"Right now, we're able to get by with fire drill management, but I can see a point in time where we're going to have to be a lot more strategic about how we take on tasks and how quickly we're able to do them," he said. Michaelson emphasized that the county does not generate data for data's own sake. That assures that data is used and the GIS system retains its credibility, he said. "We look at it from the perspective of what kinds of questions we are going to face in the future, and how we can make other departments more efficient in what they do, based on what kind of datasets we have and how accurate those sets are," he said.

Starr suggested that the county may consider developing a schedule similar to that used for its capital improvements program. Each county department and office would be asked for input on likely GIS needs and the related timeframe for each proposed use. Department heads would also be responsible for identifying available dollars within their budgets to pay for needed improvements. "The commissioners would have the final say in prioritizing the list, but we'd do it hand in glove with other elected officials [in the county]," Starr said.

Location of GIS

The county opted to use a centralized system for its GIS, and it developed it as its own department complete with assigned staff and annual budget. The GIS department falls under the long-range planning unit under the county manager's office. According to DeVore, "We made the decision to take it to the next level and make [the GIS] its own separate unit with its own resources so it wouldn't be distracted into other areas. The decision was to focus on building a system to where it was usable."

Michaelson concurred with the decision the county government made. "If every other department has its own GIS in-house, it's really hard to keep track of data integrity, and make sure everyone is using the same datasets that are the most current," he said. "With a centralized system, the GIS department can be responsible for ensuring the quality of the datasets being used instead of worrying about which department is using what datasets and the quality of that data."

To facilitate use of the system, the county stores and maintains its data on a central Web site under a contract with a regional nonprofit organization that specializes in public access to GIS data. Each county department or office has access to all the county's datasets for its own purposes. However, levels of GIS technical expertise vary across departments. "Some departments use a minimal amount of time. For others, we provide data. Some of them do it on their own. For the most part, we provide information analysis," Michaelson said.

Funding

Initial funding for the county's GIS was tied to a larger effort to upgrade its overall management information system (MIS). In 1997, the county commissioners appropriated $225,000 out of the local sales tax to make the transition from a mainframe computer using a UNIX® operating system and dumb terminals to a network of personal computers using a Windows operating system. In 1998, the commissioners spent $90,000 more to develop the GIS-based parcel mapping system, and decided on an annual investment of $100,000 for three years in the hardware needed to operate the system. Gunnison County's GIS department is relatively small compared to other counties in the area. The county employs two full-time staff members to handle GIS assignments with the department's manager contributing between 20–50 percent of his time for GIS work. Other nearby counties have staffs of between ten to twelve people in their GIS departments. Budgetary constraints are the primary reason for the difference in staff size, but Gunnison County's GIS team has also implemented a number of efficiency measures in response to the increasing demand for services. For example, new data layers are developed when the workflow is less demanding. Information analyses take precedence over other more routine tasks such as responding to data requests. Overall, Michaelson said the GIS budget is very small at approximately $150,000 annually, including staff salaries, software subscriptions, and licensing as well as all the materials associated with producing the data.

While the GIS operates as an independent department, it is closely linked to the county's larger MIS department. And funding for the MIS is unusual. Gunnison County runs its MIS as an enterprise. A users' charge is built into every county department's budget to pay for the MIS staff time as well as replacement hardware and software. There is a built-in cost to replace software and hardware every three to four years. As a result, the county has been able to keep its overall system current. Additionally, the county shows a steadier expense stream over time, and does not experience extreme spikes in individual department budgets due to large equipment or software purchases.

The GIS department also sells a significant number of maps and datasets. Michaelson said the department does "a lot of custom mapping for people, and we charge for that. And we've done a lot of digitizing work for land trusts." The mapping program brings in approximately $6,000 a year. However, as access to the GIS data is simplified through a public Web site, Michaelson expects that map sales will decrease. The program is set up to recover costs, not generate revenue for the county. Starr said, "We saw it [data sales] as an incidental benefit, but it's primarily a service we can provide to our constituents. We see this as a growing demand as more people find out about the information. It's not something we're going to be looking to for additional revenue."

Michaelson agreed. "We don't want to get in the middle of private enterprise. We have debated the issue among my staff. They said if these people will pay a thousand dollars for this CD, let's charge them a thousand dollars. But in a sense, the public has already paid for the data with their tax dollars. This is really a service we're providing to them."

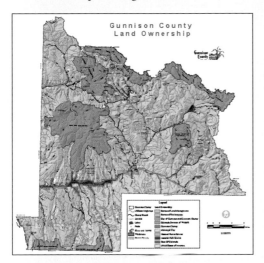

Figure 3.5 Map and data sales have offset some of the costs associated with operating Gunnison County's GIS program. This depiction of land ownership within the county is one of the more popular maps produced.

Source: Gunnison County, Colo.

Advice to other local governments

Michaelson encourages other local government officials not to get scared on the front end of building a GIS. "It takes time to build really good systems. I've seen people in such a rush to get something up and running that they make some really serious mistakes in terms of accuracy or what kind of data they have. Focus on what you want to do with the system and build around that. That's a much more efficient way to go about it," he observed.

Commissioner Starr said, from a policy point of view, elected officials need to think long term. "They need to be able to look ahead and see in five to ten years what the needs will be and types of data will be needed for the program. If they're willing to put down the money to get the system going and implemented properly, then in the long term, the GIS will save staff time," he said.

Notes

1. U.S. mining laws allow citizens and companies to establish mining claims on vacant public property to explore for minerals and to secure rights, though not ownership, to those sites. Once a mining claim has been approved, the claimant gains the right to develop and extract minerals. No other use of the land is permissible. Location notices of mining claims are normally filed with county government.

Based on information from *Circular No. 3, Mining Claims* from the Colorado Division of Minerals and Geology.

References

Baker, John C., et al. 2004. *Mapping the risks: Assessing the homeland security implications of publicly available geospatial information.* Santa Monica, Calif.: RAND Corporation-National Defense Research Institute. Available online at www.rand.org/pubs/monographs/2004/RAND_MG142.pdf.

Croswell, Peter L., and Alex Wernher. 2004. GIS program revenue generation and legal issues in public sector organizations: Results of a national survey and commentary on key issues. Washington, D.C.: Urban and Regional Information Systems Association (URISA).

Kennedy, Heather (editor). 2001. *Dictionary of GIS terminology.* Redlands, Calif.: ESRI Press.

Notes

1. Survey Analyst is an extension to ArcGIS software used to store and manage survey points, measurements, and computations.

2. While technically not correct, the terms orthophoto and aerial photo are often used interchangeably. An orthophoto has been corrected for the curvature of the earth and georeferenced to a particular location on the ground.

4

Internal business functions

Donald R. Oliver
Fire Chief, City of Wilson, North Carolina

Introduction

Local governments face a huge challenge delivering services. Increased demands from their citizens and new mandates from the federal and state governments are pushing cities and counties to provide more and more. At the same time, a general public revolt against any form of new taxes—property, sales, or otherwise—limits their ability to increase revenue. So, how does a local government do more with less? In a word, technology. And more specifically, by implementing a local government GIS.

Local governments collect enormous amounts of geographical information daily—everything from emergency service calls to building permits to voting registration and much, much more. For entirely too many local governments that is all that happens—the information is collected—end of the story. But the information holds the potential to help local governments do many things. It can evaluate programs to determine if they are realizing their goals and monitor progress toward those goals. It can analyze trends in the community. And, it can weigh the impact of different policy decisions.

Enterprise-wide GIS can significantly help local governments be more effective, efficient, and responsive in providing services to their citizenry. A GIS allows departments to assist each other in their service provision. When departments share data and information about services and infrastructure, departmental performance improves. Often one municipal department is unaware of useful data generated and maintained by another department. GIS data on the transportation system infrastructure—streets and addressing—may be developed and maintained by the public works department, but it can be of significant benefit to other departments:

- The planning department can assess growth patterns, occupancy types and usage, and traffic patterns.
- The administration department can evaluate equity in service provision, alignment and contents of voting districts, and mapping of complaints.

- The fire department can route emergency vehicles responding to calls.
- The police department can analyze crime trends and resource allocation.

Geography professor Michael N. DeMers calls GIS "an empowering technology." He likens it to the printing press, the telephone, and the automobile in terms of its long-term effect on society. "The GIS is changing the way we do things with maps, the way we think about geographic information, even the way in which geographic data are collected and compiled. Tasks that were impossible with traditional maps are now commonplace" (DeMers 1997).

In many local government departments, GIS significantly improves the workflow of daily business, and quickly demonstrates its value. This chapter highlights just a few of the many ways a GIS can enhance internal business operations in a local government. Examples of local government business areas that can increase effectiveness and efficiency with a GIS include the following:

- documentation and information efforts
- public safety and health
- environmental and land-use planning
- social and human services
- general government functions and performance management

Before exploring the efficiencies each of these areas can gain with a local government GIS, a short discussion of the challenges of implementing a GIS and a description of how a GIS works seems appropriate.

Challenges of implementing a GIS

As with any organization-wide program, procedure, or process change, implementing a GIS involves getting past some major internal and external political roadblocks.

Starting a local government GIS requires resources, both the reallocation of existing resources, particularly staff time, and the allocation of funding to purchase software and hardware. In these increasingly tight-budget times, it is difficult to convince local leaders, both internal and external, to commit resources to a new or expanded venture. Whenever government leaders are debating an investment of public dollars, they should be encouraged to consider the value of the service provided, not just the cost (Osborne and Hutchinson 2004). In this respect, a well-designed enterprise GIS will prove its worth time and again. The return on investment is often so great that the question turns from "How can we afford it?" to "How can we afford not to have it?"

Beyond the question of cost is the need to educate local government departments about GIS and how it will help staff members do their jobs better. Here, the best process for building support is to involve individual departments in designing the GIS system. Once departments understand the initial benefits, they will assist in acquiring resources for the GIS.

After the resource and departmental buy-in hurdles are cleared, another major challenge involves sharing information. To truly realize the benefits of an enterprise GIS, departments must share information. Allowing open access to departmental data is very difficult for many managers. However, information maintained or developed by one department may have significant benefit to another department. For example, the water department does not need to know the exact location and available flow from a particular hydrant, but that information is vital to the fire department in a major fire. Recognizing the critical nature of sharing accurate and up-to-date data, even if the data is only minimally important to the host department, makes it possible for all local government departments to do a better job.

Communication between departments is necessary for all parties to know the availability and importance of data. This communication can take the form of regular user group meetings or specialized training sessions. Listservs, electronic newsletters, and system bulletins also keep GIS users informed about recent developments with the system. There are many ways to keep people informed. Choose the ones that best meet the needs of the organization

Some form of centralized GIS coordination helps ensure the standardization and uniformity of data in the system. Whether a single GIS coordinator, or a GIS unit or division, specialized in-house resources greatly contribute to the usefulness and versatility of the GIS, and therefore, the benefits of the entire GIS. The commitment of senior staff, from the chief executive on down the line, is required to ensure that different departments cooperate. Just as any other asset built or purchased by a local government is government property, the data generated or maintained by a specific department truly is the property of the organization as a whole. It must be shared to ensure the maximum benefit to the organization and the community.

How GIS works

Every GIS must have a base or primary layer on which each of the additional layers can be overlaid. The additional layers are georeferenced or linked to specific geographic points or features within the basemap. In many local governments, a parcel layer serves as the base layer. The parcel layer contains graphical data—the lines that make up the boundaries of each piece of property in a jurisdiction—and tabular data—all of the relevant information about each piece of property, including parcel number, size, zoning classification, owner, and street address among other variables *(figure 4.1)*. Once the base parcel layer is created, other layers can be developed. These additional geographical layers can represent almost any physical characteristic or theme a municipality needs to display, analyze, or evaluate.

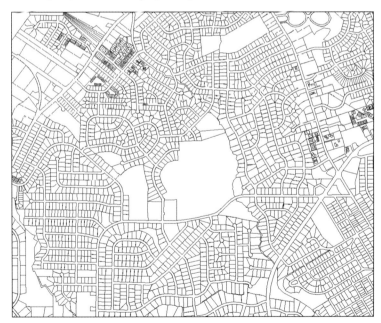

Figure 4.1   A parcel layer often serves as the foundation for building a GIS.

Source: Wilson, N.C.

Typical primary layers include streets, water lines, sewer lines, and other infrastructure-related information *(figure 4.2)*. Advanced GIS deployments have other layers such as zoning districts, census demographic data, and transportation system capacity and usage data. Other thematic layers can be developed based on the different types of data being collected by local government departments.

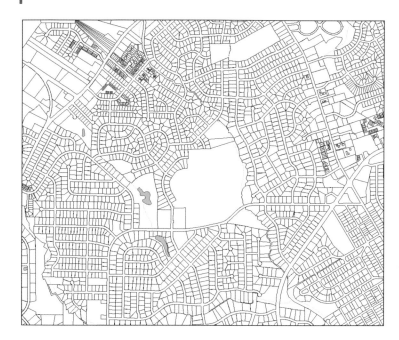

Figure 4.2 As new data layers are built for a GIS, they can be placed over the parcel layer to show new information. Here, a parcel layer is shown with street and stream layers.

Source: Wilson, N.C.

Documentation and information efforts

One of the primary functions of local government is administration (Kukay 2005). Simply put, local governments maintain records—volumes and volumes of records. The task of cataloging, storing, and retrieving paper records can be intimidating. The staff time needed to manage a paper filing system can be mammoth—not to mention the space required to retain records, especially large-scale maps like engineering diagrams and building blueprints. The security of paper records also must be considered. They can be very easily lost, damaged, or destroyed.

A GIS stores information and records it in a digital format. As a result, it takes considerably less room than paper records and maps require. The risk of losing valuable information is greatly reduced as electronic files can be easily backed up and copied. Moreover, the burden of managing the information—cataloging, storing, and retrieving—is eased since these functions are performed by the GIS electronically rather than manually. In a sense, a GIS is a type of insurance to protect a local government's permanent records.

Information stored in a GIS is also more versatile than paper records. Information gathered for a variety of purposes can be tabulated, coded, and entered into the GIS, and then used in combination with other data layers to look at the connections and better analyze what is happening on the ground. Updating records with a GIS is also substantially easier. Portable data collection units used by supervisors evaluating services, problem areas, and remote work locations can gather information off site. After the data has been uploaded into the GIS back in the office, it could be used to graphically display and analyze outcomes, performance, work plans, and resource allocation decisions. A GIS not only provides easy access to government data, it also enables the data to be manipulated for a variety of different purposes required by local government.

For example, the register of deeds, the tax office, or another support department typically develops and maintains the parcel layer. The register of deeds or other comparable office keeps the tabular data for this layer, which includes the date of most recent transfer, the sales price, and any number of other combinations or divisions of individual parcels. This layer is critical to the fundamental aspects of government and society: real property identification, valuation, transfer, and taxation. As the ad valorem property tax is a major revenue source for many local governments, developing and maintaining this information is crucial to all general governmental functions. This data is also used daily by real estate professionals in the community to determine individual property valuations and appraisal by comparison. Finally, the parcel layer data is used extensively and updated by governmental entities in their reappraisal processes.

These primary layers also provide an important foundation for creating new maps by using either existing tabular data or integrating new tabular data. For example, parcel map data can be used to generate additional layers for analyzing land use and tax base growth or decline in a community. A query can be written to select and group specific land uses to produce a community land-use map. A similar query can be created to show tax base growth or decline on a map. If historical data is available, a time trend analysis can show graphically how land use in the community has changed and how those changes relate to tax base growth or decline. Such maps provide the local government with valuable information for planning infrastructure expansions and upgrades, changing zoning districts, and expanding extraterritorial jurisdictions.

The abundant information relating to traffic patterns, volumes, and routes can be used in a GIS to aid in planning for transportation alternatives, new projects, and route development using existing infrastructure (*figure 4.3*). Most local governments either collect or have access to data on the number of users of their street systems, the times of the usage, and the patterns of usage. By combining this data with the parcel and street system geographical data, a GIS can illustrate trends in traffic problems, areas of growth in the use of traffic systems and utilities infrastructure, and how and where system improvement will be needed. These functions are also known as build-out analysis.

Figure 4.3   Mapping data on land-use patterns and major arterial streets can be used for a variety of purposes from aiding in planning transportation alternatives to route development on existing infrastructure.

Source: Wilson, N.C.

Another area that is critical to effective growth management is modeling demand and capacity trends in water and wastewater systems. The ability to analyze and model infrastructure systems is one of the many attributes that separate a GIS from a map of local infrastructure. All cities have maps of their water and wastewater systems. When these maps are incorporated into a GIS with the additional tabular data of line type and size, valve location, and topographical elevations, models can aid planning and decision making. Such models can be combined with population growth projections from the planning department to evaluate adequacy of existing systems, appropriate upgrades to systems, and locations for future facilities.

Finally, a GIS is an indispensable tool for effective economic development decision making and planning. Its ability to graphically represent a locality's infrastructure, population demographics, properties available for development, and proximity to interstate transportation systems, makes GIS a necessary component of any community's marketing strategy. Potential industrial or commercial prospects can quickly evaluate the locality's fit to its operations or services, its ability to adequately serve a new facility, and the likelihood that targeted customer or employee populations are nearby or easily accessible.

A GIS also can accurately evaluate the impact of economic development projects on service and infrastructure. Any project under consideration can be easily analyzed with a GIS to provide decision makers with an accurate picture of its total (direct and indirect) cost. Such an understanding is critical not only to the success of any given project, but to the overall economic well-being of a community.

Public safety and health

Another major responsibility of local government is public safety (Kukay 2005). It represents a substantial portion of the budget for most local governments. And since September 11, the emphasis on public safety has risen exponentially as local governments move to the frontline of defense against terrorism (Anderson 2003). But whether facing a natural or manmade disaster, local governments must be prepared to respond.

Emergency planning requires a comprehensive understanding and appreciation of the different hazards a local government is likely to experience, the resources available to respond to such events, and how resources are deployed. A GIS can greatly assist emergency planners in all of these areas. By incorporating hazardous material storage, transportation, and usage information into the GIS tabular data, planners can evaluate risk of an emergency aligned with population concentrations, land use, critical facility locations, and pre-event positioning of emergency resources.

A GIS also greatly benefits hazard evaluation and identification efforts. Existing layers such as floodplain, slope, and historical meteorological records can be combined with census demographic data to identify populations at risk from a flood or high water event. A floodplain layer can also be merged with a street system layer

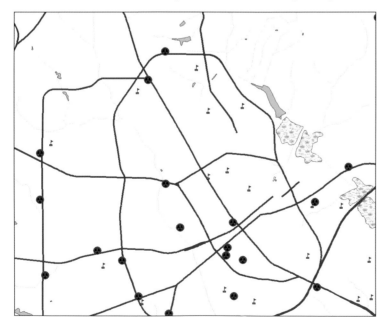

Figure 4.4   Hazard identification and evaluation are greatly aided by GIS. In this example, area schools are shown by their proximity to locations where hazardous materials are stored and the floodplains in the community.

Source: Wilson, N.C.

to identify impassable roads and alternative routes or pre-event staging areas during a flood. Information on hazardous material storage can also be compared to population and land-use information to assist in planning for evacuation areas and to identify special needs people who must be protected in place, such as hospital patients or nursing home residents.

Beyond response planning, a GIS is indispensable in mitigation and recovery planning. By assisting in the understanding of the hazards facing a community and its residents, a GIS can be of great benefit evaluating mitigation alternatives and improving recovery planning. Mitigation alternatives can be easily evaluated by how they affect populations and properties, while recovery efforts can be perfected by a more thorough understanding of a major emergency event's impact.

A myriad of data is available to local governments in relation to floodplains, flood-elevation potentials, and flood-event likelihoods. When combined with base map layers of parcels and streets, this data becomes a valuable planning tool for local governments. GIS maps can be created to illustrate at-risk populations for evacuation planning, vulnerable properties for planning and zoning regulation, and storm water infrastructure concerns for future mitigation initiatives. Local governments can further improve their flood prevention and mitigation efforts by incorporating local historical data into models to predict future storm event problems.

Public health is another area in which GIS aids understanding, evaluation, planning, and response. All local government public health departments maintain data on client concentrations and distributions. Most also maintain information related to likely public health outbreaks, methods of transmission, and resources available to respond. By using a GIS to graphically represent this information along with census demographic data, parcel data, and transportation system information data, public health officials can effectively plan their response to a public health concern, manage preventive immunization efforts, and evaluate exposure potentials.

Emergency services lead the way to enterprise GIS in Wilson, North Carolina

To demonstrate the benefits of a true enterprise approach to GIS in the City of Wilson, several small projects combined the data from multiple departments to identify and analyze systemic problems. The small demonstrations quickly turned into much larger real-world solutions that had a significant impact on the fire department's capabilities and operations.

The Wilson Fire and Rescue Services (WF/RS) knew of an area in the city where low fire hydrant pressures meant low-flow capacities. WF/RS had experienced problems during a large structure fire, and wanted to avoid similar problems. The department used a GIS application to identify the area for risk assessment and management.

In an initial fire department training session, staff from ESRI and its business partner, Omega Group, a San Diego-based GIS software developer, created a map that identified all hydrants in the city with a flow rate of less than five hundred gallons per minute by combining the fire department's hydrant testing data with the public services department's data for street and water infrastructure. Interestingly, this map was able to draw a picture of systemic problems in several areas.

Though some of this information was known to WF/RS staff members, it only had been communicated to the water department in a piecemeal work-order fashion for individual hydrants. Armed with the new GIS map, the WF/RS department and the city's risk management department were able to present local decision makers with a clear picture of the problem.

The results were immediate and very effective. The city installed new water mains in several areas, updated hydrants, and reappropriated a large "loop line" project that had been removed from the budget.

Prepared by Donald R. Oliver, fire chief for the City of Wilson, N.C.

The benefits of an enterprise GIS deployment do not stop at the planning stages. Rather they are just beginning. Once an emergency event occurs, emergency responders can use a GIS to improve their understanding of affected and exposed populations and properties, and locations of resources available to mitigate damage from the event. An emergency responder's ability to understand the magnitude of the event and the available resources helps minimize loss of life and property. A GIS can help an incident commander develop and manipulate map layers in real time to manage resources very effectively in ongoing emergency operations.

Environment and land use

The demand for parks and recreation facilities and programs has increased remarkably over the last two decades. Desire for public green spaces has also grown as public attention has focused on maintaining healthy lifestyles and enhancing overall quality of life. This area of local government management is an ideal fit for a GIS. An early GIS was designed for natural resource and land-use management. The Canada Geographic Information System was developed by the Canadian Department of Forestry and Rural Development at the beginning of the 1960s. "Its initial task was to classify and map the land resources of Canada" (DeMers 1997).

A GIS can help evaluate locations for new facilities, assess renovation alternatives for existing facilities, and determine locations for programs. Parks and recreation managers use existing base parcel layers, transportation system layers, census demographic layers, and projected growth pattern layers from the planning department, to evaluate existing facilities for ease of access, proximity to demand populations, and capacity requirements. A GIS can quickly and effectively illustrate demand concentrations for programming and contrast them with locations of facilities and programs. By incorporating planning for parks and recreational facilities in strategic planning initiatives, local governments can proactively prepare for growth and thus be more responsive to citizens' needs.

GIS plays a crucial role in analyzing the suitable location or relocation of parks and other recreational facilities and identifying environmentally sensitive areas for preservation purposes. GIS explores not only the *what*, *where*, and *when*, but also the *what if*, through suitability analysis. For example, a GIS can be especially useful for determining where green space should be developed in the community. Taking predefined criteria required as buffer space between industrial and other zoning districts, a GIS can analyze the area needed for green space. Similarly, a GIS can show areas along rivers and other waterways that would be best left as green space in the event of flooding.

GIS has often gotten its start in a local government in the areas of land use, planning, zoning, and engineering. Many times, in fact, it is seen as the exclusive domain of those fields (chapter 2). Nonetheless, GIS applications in these areas have a profound influence on the ability of a local government to respond to and establish policy for community development. Land-use and zoning data in a GIS can be used to show how and where land is being used within the community. The modeling capabilities of a GIS are particularly valuable for this purpose as they can quickly and easily show alternative development scenarios, allowing policy makers to see immediately the impact of decisions. The power of a GIS can also be used to help set priorities for action as the case study on Philadelphia's housing demolition program illustrates.

Social and human services

Local governments provide a tremendous number of social and human services, and demand for those services continues to grow whether it is families in crisis, troubled youth, or employment services and job training. The use of a GIS to improve service delivery in this area is relatively new, but mapping the location of services

Demolition decisions in Philadelphia, Pennsylvania

Launched in 2000, the Neighborhood Transformation Initiative in Philadelphia addresses the challenges of blight caused by dangerous buildings and vacant properties as part of its goal to rebuild and revitalize neighborhoods. A 2001 survey showed that the city had nearly 8,000 buildings that were imminently dangerous, and 60,000 vacant lots and buildings. Establishing a plan to undertake such a massive demolition effort would not have been possible without the power of a GIS.

The city chose to use its GIS as the foundation of a decision support system (DSS) to assist in this enormous endeavor. Drawing on the city's existing digital data, the DSS uses a computer model to evaluate the demolition and stabilization needs of a neighborhood and to compare those needs with the redevelopment and rehabilitation opportunities available. Different city departments supplied data to build the computer model. The mayor's Office of Information Services provided information about land parcels, census tracts, street networks, water bodies, and schools. Data on dangerous buildings and vacant structures came from the Licenses and Inspections Department; publicly owned buildings from the Bureau of Revenue and Taxes; and housing markets from the redevelopment fund.

Using pre-defined decision criteria for ten variables, the decision makers weighed the importance of the criteria based on their district's or neighborhood's needs and vision for redevelopment activities. The computer model runs the scenario and then displays the results as a color-coded map layer. This allows local government officials to see the results of their decisions immediately. For example, an official can see which buildings should be demolished if she assigns more weight to the condition of the vacant structure than its proximity to elementary schools. This tool greatly speeds the decision-making process, and produces maps of potential properties for demolition instantaneously. The GIS application allows planning to move forward faster, more reliably, and more cost effectively in a comprehensible fashion.

Based on "GIS as bulldozer: Using GIS for a massive urban demolition project," by Dr. Yongmin Yan and Kevin Switala, a paper presented at the 2002 ESRI International User Conference, July 8–12 in San Diego, Calif.

relative to needs within the community has proven its value to local policy makers as the Lee County, Florida, case study on page 70 illustrates.

Most social services departments already maintain manual or digital databases on client locations, concentrations, and types of service demand. If this information is entered into a GIS and combined with existing map layers, social services officials can easily evaluate demand concentrations versus service locations as well as service demand location trends to aid in planning. They can also review the types of services provided as they relate to the clients' locations. For example, all social services agencies maintain client addresses and other records. Social services agencies can use the power of GIS to map out the location of their clients and overlay this new layer to analyze the proximity of clients to transit routes or identify clusters of clients in relationship to work centers or service locations.

Using GIS for human services delivery in Lee County, Florida

The Lee County Department of Human Services (DHS) supports low-income county residents with a wide variety of programs. Everything from housing and targeted neighborhood development to vocational training to HIV/AIDS support falls under its purview. The department also administers a number of state-mandated programs in public health, mental health, and substance abuse. But delivery of human services goes well beyond the programs and services that DHS provides. Lee County also has an extensive network of other government agencies, nonprofit organizations, and faith-based groups offering such programs. With so many programs and players operating in the county, planning and integrating strategies had to be coordinated to ensure funding was directed where needed and scarce resources allocated efficiently.

A DHS team determined that a GIS could display the multiple demographic, time, and location needs of the community with the human services programs available. The team developed a comprehensive strategy for using GIS in three major phases: demonstration, collaborative implementation, and public use. During the demonstration phase, DHS brought together its staff as well as representatives from collaborating agencies to discuss GIS needs and objectives. Based on the feedback received, the agency developed a request for proposals to prepare four human services GIS projects: affordable housing, community health, neighborhood development, and human services provider locations.

After hiring a consultant, work began on the four model demonstration maps. The purpose of the maps was to showcase how a GIS analysis could compare one set of parameters with another. For example, the affordable housing map compares income categories in the county to the range of area rents. The maps enable human services providers to see within the county where the human services needs are the greatest or where gaps may exist. Graphically depicting where problems exist in the county has helped the vast network of human services providers improve programs that better respond to needs within the county.

Based on "Human services delivery with GIS, Initial steps, Lee County, Florida" by Richard Faris, John Bizelli, Amy Hoyt, and Courtney Sullivan, a paper presented at the 2004 ESRI International User Conference, August 9–13, 2004 in San Diego, Calif.

Social service organizations can also benefit from existing GIS data layers. Most planning and inspection departments maintain databases of housing stocks available in a community. A GIS can combine these layers to evaluate the proximity of available rental and for-purchase properties to existing demand populations, work centers, and shopping center concentrations. A GIS can also help planning agencies, community land trusts, and social service agencies evaluate the supply of suitable housing for redevelopment by contrasting housing stock layers with concentrations of population demand for housing.

General government functions and performance management

The finance department and elections office are among the more general local government functions that benefit from GIS. Finance departments use GIS in their capital asset reporting requirements, such as those contained in the new model of the Governmental Accounting Standards Board (GASB) Statement No. 34. A properly implemented GIS will contain tabular data supporting shape, line, and point layers that document a local government's infrastructure—essentially most of their capital assets. By including information relative to the date of installation or construction, initial cost, and current value, to the physical specification and description of the asset or infrastructure item, a GIS can help the finance department accurately report the local government's assets and liabilities. With a GIS, a description of a fixed or capital asset can be transformed from an entry on a financial statement to a graphical and spatial depiction of the asset, its use, and its value. The actions of the operating departments in the maintenance, construction, and infrastructure replacement items, when appropriately documented in the GIS, allow the finance department to determine more accurately the financial condition of the entity.

Coordinating infrastructure improvements in San Diego, California

Like the vast majority of cities across the country, San Diego operates a capital improvement program (CIP) to maintain and improve the quality of the various infrastructure systems. Many of the CIP projects involve pipelines or other work affecting public right-of-way on the city streets. These projects, along with road maintenance and other resurfacing, require coordination. In response, the city developed San Diego City-Works, a GIS application that provides easy-to-use, up-to-date information on what CIP projects are underway or planned for any given area of the city and when.

San Diego CityWorks began as a multidepartment project designed to merge several separate efforts in different departments. The San Diego CityWorks application uses data from the CIP plan as well as the following sources:
- water infrastructure
- sewer infrastructure
- public facilities
- ADA-compliant ramps
- pavement projects
- streets
- natural features
- community planning areas
- council districts
- park and recreation centers
- orthophotos

By combining this data, the GIS can produce a master overview of what is happening where and when within the city regarding infrastructure improvements. Using this standard citywide process, San Diego City-Works enables better coordination and communication among project managers in various city departments. By working in a more coordinated fashion, the impact of CIP projects on the public—and its ability to move around the city—is significantly minimized.

Rod Greek, City of San Diego, and Chrispyle, San Diego Data Processing Corporation

Local governments can also use GIS for better asset management in general. Asset management emphasizes strategic decision making to maximize the benefits and minimize the costs of physical assets. The process requires proactive and predictive investment, maintenance, rehabilitation, and replacement. Better maintenance of a community's infrastructure can substantially extend its lifetime. A GIS can help by identifying the location of assets, recording asset attributes such as location, size, age, system condition, and recent maintenance. With this information, public works employees can determine the best course of action for scheduling maintenance and replacing infrastructure based on an analysis using predetermined selection criteria.

The operations of elections offices of most local governments are consumed with the correct registration of voters and the accounting of ballots in any given election. Key to this process is the districting and redistricting of voters in a given geographical, or in this case, political area. A GIS benefits this process and the operation of the elections office by combining the information from the voter registration information with the spatial information of the parcel layer, and tabular data from the U.S. Bureau of the Census. Through GIS, any geographic area and its inhabiting population can be analyzed, and divided or redistricted by race, political affiliation, sex, socioeconomic level, family size, creed, or any other determinate gathered by the U.S. Census. The ability to accurately divide and redistrict populations has aided many jurisdictions in complying with U.S. Department of Justice regulations and orders.

As noted at the beginning of this chapter, local government budgets are increasingly tight. Many local governments have responded to this pressing challenge by instituting performance management systems for their departments. Performance management systems enable governments to make funding decisions based on

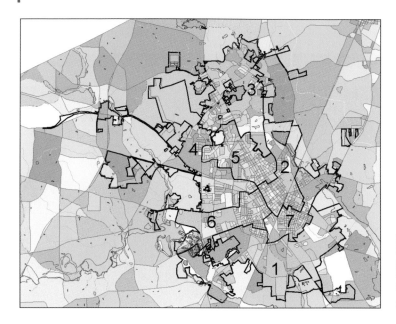

Figure 4.5 GIS assists local governments in improving voter registration records and can speed the redistricting process by quickly displaying alternative plans for redistricting based on various criteria.

Source: Wilson, N.C.

sound financial analysis and to target their limited resources toward productive programs. The systems gather various performance data as indicators of effectiveness, and use trend analysis to inform local government officials and managers who allocate resources and make decisions. These systems determine if programs are achieving the desired results and meeting the needs of the public. The in-depth case study accompanying this chapter discusses integrating GIS with a performance management system in the municipality of Chatham-Kent, Ontario, in Canada.

A local government GIS can contribute greatly to identifying trends and monitoring progress toward goals. GIS can show, for example, if crime in a given neighborhood is decreasing as a result of more police patrols. It can demonstrate if a new zoning ordinance permitting increased density in residential neighborhoods has resulted in more affordable housing. Or it can determine if pest control procedures are helping to control disease outbreaks in the community. Once a community has established goals using an investment of taxpayer dollars, a GIS can help track the results as part of a performance management system.

Final thoughts

The gamut of local government programs and services has expanded considerably in the past few decades. Elected officials and department managers struggle to stay ahead of the game and continue to provide the quality programs and services their citizens want and deserve. It is a hard task and requires new skills and tools to achieve ever greater levels of effectiveness and efficiency. The investment in local government GIS is no small undertaking and needs to be discussed and debated thoroughly by local decision makers. But it is a tool that is revolutionizing the internal business operations of local government.

This chapter has discussed just a few of the ways a GIS can be used to improve the daily operations of local government. Many more exist, and many more will be developed in the coming years. The question is not whether a local government GIS is a worthwhile investment, but rather how to make the investment.

Chatham-Kent, Ontario, Canada

Profile—Municipal government	
Location	Southwestern Ontario
Size (miles square)	2,494 square kilometers (962.94 square miles)
Population	110,000
Form of government	Council-manager
Annual GIS operating budget	Can$350,000 for municipal GIS and Can$450,000 for utility's AM/FM system
Employees in GIS units	3.5 FTEs in municipal GIS and 2.5 FTEs in utility's AM/FM system
Governmental departments using GIS	10

Overview

In 1998, twenty-three communities in southwestern Ontario, Canada, merged to become a single-tier municipality. This case study focuses on how Chatham-Kent's GIS helped the new municipality improve its overall efficiency and provide better service to its customers.

Background

GIS started in Chatham-Kent in 1998 when the municipality's public utility commission (PUC) partnered with a local gas utility company, Union Gas, a division of Duke Energy, to do asset mapping of electric, water, and wastewater infrastructure in the area. The mapping effort converted into a digital format all available paper records and engineering drawings with utility information, such as sewers and water lines. The PUC also collected all the attributes associated with the various infrastructure systems, and stored those in a GIS database. The resulting enterprise GIS, known as the AM/FM system, established a series of basic data layers for the municipality. Before the Chatham-Kent project, Union Gas had successfully completed a similar effort for its entire gas network across Ontario. "We had a great partnership. Union Gas provided Chatham-Kent with one of their technical staff members who had the needed expertise, and we paid the salary," said Mayor Diane Gagner.

Meanwhile, the local government began to develop a strategic plan for an enterprise-wide GIS. Municipal executives hoped to leverage the work the PUC had already done in building the AM/FM system. The project was initially managed by Union Gas staff, but was turned over to municipal staff during the early stages of the enterprise GIS project.

The utility-based AM/FM system provided the municipality with a foundation layer of data. "We developed our initial land base, our parcel fabric, our street line networks, and all of the electric, water, and wastewater infrastructure data that's in the system," said Jeff Ham, manager of corporate applications under Chatham-Kent's information technology services. In 2002, the municipal council approved plans for a municipal GIS that built upon the basic data layers from the AM/FM system, and included new data layers with more land-based and parcel information. Among other features, the new system was designed to marry the existing data with tax assessment data and property ownership records. The three-year project wrapped up at the end of 2004. The municipality joined with ESRI business partner, Orion Technology, Inc., of Richmond Hill, Ontario, Canada, to rapidly implement this project.

Besides investing its own money, Chatham-Kent secured grant funds from the provincial government in Ontario to support its GIS development. The Ontario Ministry of Natural Resources provided about Can$1.5 million toward the municipality's GIS and other information technology initiatives, including a

Web portal to allow the public to log in and view GIS data. The funding came in the form of a 1:1 matching grant that required Chatham-Kent to spend Can$1.5 million of its own funds.

Improving operations

Chatham-Kent's GIS allows the municipality to provide a series of common datasets to all local government departments. Staff has a single, up-to-date source for address and location information within the community. It also enables the municipality to make more datasets available. As each department creates new datasets, they are shared with all the other government departments. In short, everyone has access to more and better information.

Aileen Murray, manager of business retention and attraction services within Chatham-Kent's economic development services, said the GIS has helped her department deliver information to its clients quickly. She also found that her department's internal expectations of how fast staff can provide information to clients has changed drastically. "Just five years ago, it used to take one week to pull together some pretty tedious data for a client. Now it takes maybe an hour," she said.

Figure 4.6 Chatham-Kent has found GIS technology especially useful for its economic development efforts. Staff can gather data and respond to client inquiries in a matter of hours instead of days as result.

Source: Municipality of Chatham-Kent, centre for GIS

GIS has changed the way Chatham-Kent collects information. Murray said a GIS requires standards for data collection and forces people to be more accurate. For example, it is not sufficient to list a street intersection as an address, but rather the full street address must be recorded. As a result, ". . .we had to be a little bit more disciplined about how we collected and maintained site information," she said. Ham added that the GIS has made staff aware that keeping information up-to-date is important. New procedures capture and maintain information when new infrastructure is installed.

Murray described the change as a cultural shift: "Within local government, we had to come to appreciate that the data wasn't going to sit in a paper file anymore. The primary way of maintaining it was going to be electronic. . . and we had to develop an appreciation for why it had to be in a standardized format for recording that information."

Cooperation among departments

Chatham-Kent has always enjoyed good working relationships among its different departments, but GIS solidifies that cooperation, said Mayor Gagner. "You're getting people in the same room at the same time, and I think it facilitates joint decision-making processes. . .and the GIS provides factual information for their work on specific cross-cutting issues affecting the community."

Murray's department has worked very closely with Ham's department on developing specific GIS applications. But she finds she is interacting less with some departments as a result of GIS. "We don't need to bother the wastewater folks as much because we can access their information ourselves on the GIS," she said.

Data layers for Chatham-Kent's GIS are designed to be applicable to as many departments as possible. Ham said the most used and most popular data layers maintained include the following:
- streetline center data, referred to as Single Line Road Network (SLRN)
- address layer with address points
- aerial photographs
- parcel or property information
- landownership

Most municipal departments will likely use one or more of these layers in their specific business applications.

Ham said many departments are surprised to learn that other business areas within local government have an interest in their data. The building or planning department, for example, creates an address for a new lot, but that address is also important to emergency services and the 911 dispatch system, he said. "That part of the business process was not clear to all the different departmental stakeholders until we all started sharing the same GIS address database," Ham said.

Introducing staff to the GIS

Transitioning into using the new GIS applications was no problem for Chatham-Kent. Municipal employees saw it as a positive development. Ham said, "People were hungry for it, very hungry for it. In fact, it was a case of managing high expectations, because we were spending a fair amount of money on implementing this system that was hopefully going to make people's lives a little easier in terms of accessing information and being able to do their jobs better."

Training about four hundred staff members to use the new system was a critical component of the GIS implementation plan at Chatham-Kent. About twenty-five staff members from different departments participated in a pilot training on using the Web-enabled enterprise GIS application. Feedback from these sessions helped develop a standard corporate GIS training program to rollout to all staff. More than two hundred staff members were trained during twenty consecutive daily training sessions held in the fall of 2002. About twenty staff members are trained at sessions held every two months.

Tips on data management

Managing GIS data is a substantial ongoing task. Ham and Murray agreed that a fair amount of research and forethought should go into developing the procedures for acquiring and updating data for a GIS. For the wastewater department, Ham's team developed standard paper forms for workers to use while they are in the field. After workers finish installing new lines, they record information about the line on the forms and bring the forms into the office where the data is entered into the GIS.

Developing solid models for using the data can help drive home the importance of following the processes, according to Ham. "I found that departments are very excited when you actually start to see the models," he said. "That's where the GIS begins to turn on lights, and they realize what they can use it for down the road." Understanding the benefits of a GIS, he said, convinces staff to take ownership of the processes needed to keep information up-to-date. "Staff have begun to realize that what they put into it is what they're going to get out of it," he said.

At the same time, Ham advised against getting too caught up in cleaning data for the GIS. While having accurate data is important, he said, ". . .if you wait until it's perfect, you'll never get done. It's a bit of an 80–20 rule. You want to get it to where it's 80 percent there, and then spend the rest of the time fixing the remaining 20 percent. But you have to draw a line in the sand some place because you need to get something up and running that's useful."

GIS and performance management

Mayor Gagner emphasized the role of GIS in improving efficiencies within local government as a means for improving customer relations. She described the municipality's intent to more tightly integrate the GIS with the municipality's performance management system, Chatham-Kent Tracking Results And Achieving eXcellence or CK TRAAX. The system is used to track the performance and response times of government departments when they receive a complaint or call for assistance from a resident.

For instance, a resident's complaint about a pothole is entered into the system and assigned a ticket number. After that, the ticket is sent to the appropriate department to do the work. Once the department has addressed the issue, the ticket number is closed. Municipal staff members also follow up with the customer who reported the problem. At each step in the process, however, there are expected timeframes and targets for response. The municipal council schedules regular meetings with the department heads, referred to as CK TRAAX accountability sessions, to review the departmental reports. If a department is not meeting its targets, it needs to explain why not. Assignments are made to resolve any identified problems.

Integrating this performance management system more tightly with the GIS will enable the city to locate problem sites throughout the community, and assign resources where most needed. "Instead of sending someone out to fix one pothole on a street today, and then out again to fix another one around the corner tomorrow, we're taking care of all of them in a given location at the same time," said Mayor Gagner. "So what you're doing is improving the turnaround time for the customer and better utilizing the resources, the people, and the equipment you have available to do the job."

Advice for other local governments

Ham offered three key steps for implementing a local government GIS. First, identify an executive-level manager to sponsor or promote the system. This person needs to be willing to stick his or her neck out a bit to make change happen. Second, develop a strategy and implementation plan for the GIS and then have all levels of the organization sign off on the plan. This creates greater awareness of how and when the system will be put into place. Finally, set up a solid project plan and then implement it. Once the projects are up and running, interest in the system will increase exponentially.

a.

b.

Figure 4.7a and b Chatham-Kent staff uses a Web-enabled GIS tool to query data sets over the municipality's intranet. This system will interface with a performance management system, CKTRAAX, to enable the municipality to allocate resources more efficiently for infrastructure repairs and preventive maintenance.

Source: Municipality of Chatham-Kent, centre for GIS

Mayor Gagner encouraged local governments to show benefits of the system that are meaningful to the average person. "A techie person can get all excited and talk to someone about the technical end of the system, but you really need to bring it down and explain it in a way that my grandmother could understand. . . . If it is too highly technical, you're going to lose them. That's how you present it to the public and to the council," she said.

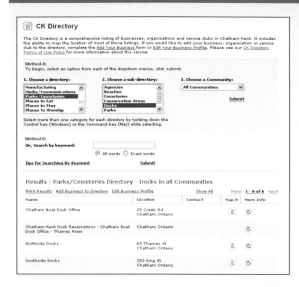

a.

b.

Figure 4.8a and b Chatham-Kent maintains a business directory within its GIS that allows users to query for places of interest, then locate the sites on a map using a simple "map-it" button.

Source: Municipality of Chatham-Kent, centre for GIS

Chapter 4

References

Anderson, Brian. 2003. *Call to action: Executive guide for homeland security—local government critical infrastructure assurance.* Washington, D.C.: Public Technology, Inc.

DeMers, Michael N. 1997. *Fundamentals of geographic information systems.* New York, N.Y.: John Wiley and Sons, Inc.

Kukay, Nancy. 2005. *The impact of devolution. A primer on local government.* Bucyrus, Ohio: Ohio State University Extension. Available online at crawford.osu.edu/cd/cd/myweb2/a_primer_on_local_government.htm.

Osborne, David, and Peter Hutchinson. 2004. *The price of government: Getting the results we need in an age of permanent fiscal crisis.* New York, N.Y.: Basic Books.

5

External services

Linda Gerull
GIS Manager, Pierce County, Washington

Why external services?

The previous chapters described how GIS has significantly changed local government business practices and information systems. GIS technology has grown well beyond a single planner performing analysis to a strategic information system integrated into the daily process of government business. With GIS, local governments can achieve tangible benefits that justify the resources and time needed to implement spatial data processing.

Another significant technology has expanded the scope and usefulness of GIS—the Internet. The combination of GIS and the Internet, along with mobile technologies and wireless data transmission linked to large databases, will connect citizens with their government in ways unthinkable just ten years ago.

GIS offers possibilities that go beyond the confines of government offices and internal computer networks. This chapter on external services describes how GIS can provide public services, improve communications and cooperation between government agencies, streamline business processes, and increase citizen participation in governance. The types of external services that are ideally suited to GIS include the following:

- e-government enabled with GIS
- regional GIS services
- public subscription services
- licensing or transfer of software
- digital data services
- mapping, consulting, and training services
- Web application services

Not every local government can provide all of these services; some require greater levels of expertise and experience than are readily available. But they underscore the diversity of options and the importance of creativity when implementing a GIS. Because this is such a new field for many organizations, this chapter describes current practices for offering these external services, guidelines for pricing services, and suggested terms and conditions for use.

Background

What factors are driving the demand for external services in local government?

- As governments build information systems, the line between internal government business functions and public access to information is blurring. For example, many citizens want
  - to access their permit status without driving to the permit office
  - an opportunity to comment on council meeting items without attending the meeting
  - information on sex offenders in an area without calling law enforcement
- Local issues such as flooding, crime, transportation, and land-use planning do not follow jurisdictional boundaries, and citizens desire a holistic approach to problem solving that requires governments to work together. GIS can provide a common view that can be shared among multiple agencies, facilitating cooperation and collaboration.
- Budgets are tight, and sharing resources between agencies can lower costs.
- Responsive government includes providing good customer service, which can be improved with Internet-based systems that are accessible twenty-four hours a day and seven days a week.
- Citizens want government to offer the same information services and digital payment options as commercial business.
- Citizens are eager to participate and assist government agencies in planning, reporting crime, and identifying needed repairs to roads or storm drains. By providing information and involving citizens, misinformation is reduced, problems are more quickly resolved, and citizens learn about government's role, constraints, and costs.

What is most interesting about these new opportunities is the relatively low cost of offering external services and their corresponding high benefits. With very little capital investment, existing data systems can be used in innovative ways as an external service. In some cases, these services can generate new revenue that offset the cost of providing the service. Based on the experiences of GIS organizations offering external services, they rarely equal or exceed that cost. External services must be justified based on organizational benefits. Any revenue is a bonus.

Just as starting an internal GIS requires a champion (chapter 3) to envision the benefits of GIS and apply the technology, external services require executive-level political support. External services can change the way government staff members relate to citizens, businesses, and other governments. This level of change does draw detractors. When faced with reviewing a contract for external services, an attorney for a large county questioned, "Where in the county charter does it say that we should be providing digital services?" Change happens, and this chapter reviews various types of external services, the benefits associated with the services, implementation strategies, opportunities to generate revenue, and associated legal issues.

E-government services enabled with GIS

Two commonly used terms for local government's use of Internet technology are e-government (electronic government) and digital government services. GIS has an important role to play in e-government for two reasons. First, approximately 80 percent of government data records can be geographically referenced (GAO 2003). This allows records to be searched by geographic identifiers such as address, parcel number, intersection, or plat name, then located and mapped by a Web application using GIS. Secondly, an easy way for citizens to access and visualize spatial information is with a map. A Web-based map display or interactive mapping system is a very intuitive and effective way to inform, educate, and communicate information about how crime, land-use changes, annexations, or road closures will affect a community.

E-government can be enhanced with GIS functions to

- Display interactive maps to view various map layers singularly or combined.
- Query the map display and report specific information about features such as parcels or zoning.
- Spatially locate and display unique information such as a parcel by parcel number, streets by name, or survey control monument by monument number.
- Perform spatial analysis to find the closest park or all crime within a distance from an address, or property sales comparables in a neighborhood.
- Navigate users to associated data by linking information to the map display. For example, a Web-based map can show the impact of a new development on surrounding land use, and the map can be used to link to other documents such as construction plans, permits, meeting notes from the land-use advisory board, or the environmental impact review document.

Any local government department can implement these GIS functions in its Internet applications. GIS adds value by providing mapping, analysis, reporting, and locating functionality. Table 1 provides examples of how various local government departments use GIS in Web applications.

The uses for GIS in e-government and Internet applications are unlimited, as are the benefits to citizens and government. Several clear benefit trends stand out to justify GIS in e-government Web sites. Benefits for citizens focus on the intrinsic value of place, for example:

- A more personalized way to search for information using addresses to find permits, utility information, property taxes, and hazards.

Table 5.1 Leading practices for enhancing e-government with GIS		
Local government	Description of e-government service	GIS-enhanced application
Assessor	Provide property information on the Web.	Display a map of the property, view lot dimensions, orthophotos, and other data layers.
	Include property record (land and structures), tax summary/history and a property sales comparative search.	Click on parcel in the map and display property record information. GIS data analysis can determine property sales comparables within a neighborhood or appraisal area.
Auditor	List polling locations on the Web.	Use an address search to geocode the location and display the precinct map and poll location.
	Provide election results on the Web.	Display maps of election results by precinct or for entire jurisdiction. This is especially useful for voter initiative results.
Public works	Create a Web-based service request system for reporting potholes, clogged drains or other maintenance items.	Use GIS to help citizens locate the address of a service request and display a map so users can identify where the problem is occurring.
	Provide survey monument information on the Web.	Search by address, monument number, or intersection to view an interactive GIS map display of survey monuments, orthophotos, and contours. Click on the survey monument in the map to view a full monument report.
Transportation services	Provide yearly information on road improvements on the Web to shows capital projects and road closures.	Enhance tabular information with an interactive map display of where capital transportation projects will be performed and click on a project to view details and budget information.
	Provide information on transportation improvement plans for the next 10 years.	Include a GIS window to display transportation plans and link projects described in the plan document (PDF) to the map window.

Local government	Description of e-government service	GIS-enhanced application
Table 5.1 Leading practices for enhancing e-government with GIS (cont.)		
Planning	Provide building permit information such as status, details and next steps. Document zoning regulations and critical area information that could affect a permit.	Use GIS to query by address, parcel number or permit number and view GIS data layers such as zoning, environmental factors and parcels. Link zoning regulations to a GIS map display of where this zoning is located. Use GIS to produce cartographic maps of land information and post in downloadable format.
Emergency management	Provide emergency information on the Web to improve public safety.	Use GIS to display interactive maps of evacuation routes, road closures, and hazard areas (floods, mud flows). Use GIS capabilities to provide up-to-date map information to first responders.
Law enforcement	Per Megan's Law, provide information about sex offenders on the Web. Provide statistical information about crime in neighborhoods.	With GIS, citizens can search by address and display information about sex offenders living within a distance from a location. GIS spatial analysis can be used to summarize crime reports for a neighborhood or in proximity to an address.
Community services Human services	Provide listing of human resources on the Web	Using GIS, citizens can search by address and report types of resources within a distance from an address. Viewing maps and bus stop locations linked to transit route information can assist with transportation needs.
Parks	Provide a listing of parks and recreation facilities on the Web.	GIS can add an interactive map showing park locations linked to recreation information as well as allow citizens to search for parks with a proximity to a location.
Economic development	Promote the community's economic development by showcasing job opportunities, housing, recreation, transportation, and community resources.	GIS can be used to add a visual component to tables and charts. Interactive mapping can display available retail or industrial space, parks, transportation, and schools. GIS search capabilities can allow businesses to query census information, demographics, and property data to help locate a new facility.
General	Additional uses for e-government not department specific.	Use GIS to provide public information and interactive mapping to locate the closest recycling center, view garbage routes, map firearm restricted zones, report government leaders by address, publish adopted plans/maps, and communicate specific information by address.

- Understanding the spatial relationships within communities to make better decisions, such as the location of flood zones, new construction, human services, hazards, and traffic congestion.
- Location-based information allows citizens to make better decisions, such as how to avoid traffic congestion.

Benefits for government focus on data accuracy, relevant public comment, and time savings, for example:

- Participation in government increases by providing maps and analysis online for comment and feedback. Citizens viewing maps can see issues that will affect them directly, which improves the quality of public comment.
- Citizens reporting the specific location of potholes or service requests saves staff time, and it is more efficient when staff can review the proximity of one call to another and plan work expeditiously.
- The quality of online databases and maps are improved as citizens report discrepancies or mistakes in the data.

- Visits to government offices are reduced while service is increased. Local business can be supported when external GIS Web services allow them to
  - access survey data needed for survey and engineering firms
  - research property records and maps required by title companies
  - secure permit records and conduct critical data analysis needed by engineering and construction operations
  - collect site location information needed by industrial consultants or large companies to accurately assess and evaluate a locality

Citizens and government benefit when GIS is a component in external e-government Web sites. The applications and services will dramatically increase as government leaders and information technology departments see the value of communicating directly with citizens via interactive maps.

Finding new ways to serve the public with GIS in Lucas County, Ohio

In 1993, the Lucas County Auditor's Office maintained five different data systems to assess the nearly 200,000 parcels in the county. The multiple systems made compiling data on a specific piece of property a cumbersome process. It was difficult to respond to inquiries from the public in a timely fashion. To better serve the public, the Auditor's Real Estate Information System (AREIS) was developed. AREIS fully integrated the five different data systems into one GIS with five primary applications:

- Front Counter
- AREIS Online
- AREIS CD/DVD
- MAPrint
- ARFIS Express

The Front Counter application offers the fastest access to current real estate data, and allows area residents to look up information on parcels within the county. A simple-to-use search function enables the user to search by address, assessor number, or parcel number. Once a search has been performed, the user can gather data on land features:

- attributes
- general property data, including ownership and value/tax information
- ownership history
- terrestrial structure image
- building footprint sketch

AREIS Online *(www.lucascountyoh.gov/AREIS/areismain.asp)* allows for real-time access to transfer information, maps and tax data. Sales, ownership, payments, and tax accounting records can be pulled directly from the county's real estate databases. Also available through AREIS Online are transfer card images, structure photos, and structure sketches.

A new AREIS CD/DVD is issued quarterly and provides information similar to that found on AREIS Online. AREIS CD/DVD comes with expanded mapping and spatial analysis capabilities. For example, the county's flood insurance rate map index has been incorporated into the CD/DVD, enabling the user to reference properties and buildings to determine the potential risk of flood damage based on historic, meteorological, hydrologic, and hydraulic data. The comparable sales wizard is one of the most popular features. With this feature, the user can search for residential and non-residential property by year built, occupancy, construction type, square footage, sale year, or sale price.

Finding new ways to serve the public with GIS in Lucas County, Ohio (cont.)

MAPrint re-creates the county's old Mylar® tax maps in a digital format. The public can have custom map printing completed in a matter of minutes using the application. The maps are available in sizes ranging from 8 1/2 by 11 inches to 34 by 44 inches with or without aerial photos.

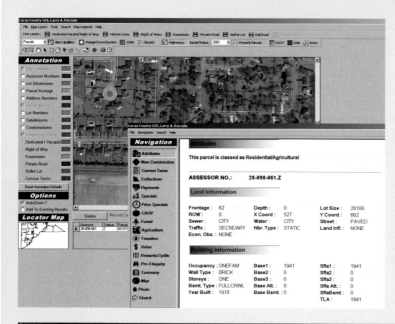

Figure 5.1 Lucas County provides a variety of business services to its residents through Web-based and client/server GIS applications. The Front Counter Application provides an integrated interface to real estate information, including tax records, appraisal data, mapping, front structure photos, property sketches, and historical documents.

Source: Lucas County, Ohio

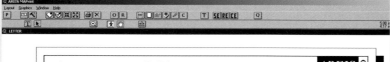

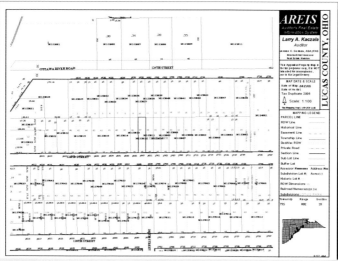

Figure 5.2 On January 1, 2001, the Lucas County Auditor's Office went live with AREIS MAPrint, a virtual, real-time version of the county tax map. MAPrint replaced historical Mylar maps with digitally created, customized tax maps.

Source: Lucas County, Ohio

Finding new ways to serve the public with GIS in Lucas County, Ohio (cont.)

AREIS Express is the newest application the county has put in place. The application uses public kiosks with a touch screen to give residents quick and easy access to a variety of information such as the location of easements or zoning classifications affecting their property. Residents can also use the kiosks to print out maps of their neighborhoods.

According to Lucas County Auditor Larry A. Kaczala, "We are in the business of public service, and continually strive to increase awareness of the AREIS products. The information offered by AREIS gives the public greater knowledge of Lucas County real estate, as well as a means to verify their own property data, thereby ensuring a fair and equitable tax value."

Based on "GIS serving the public: Past, present, and future in Lucas County" by Randy Schardt and Brian Sovik, as presented at the 2004 ESRI International User Conference, August 9-13, 2004 in San Diego, Calif.

Public subscription services

An interesting trend in e-government is subscription services to local government's Web applications. In rushing to embrace the Internet, governments have focused on having a Web presence, providing direct access to databases, and inventing new services for citizens. These initiatives led to the development of impressive Web sites. But as government's use of the Internet has expanded, the reality of supporting and maintaining a rapidly growing and often complex set of Web applications is breaking budgets. As a result, some local governments have begun to offer public subscription services to offset GIS maintenance costs. Individuals pay a fee to access select GIS applications or databases.

Innovative e-government applications using GIS require bandwidth, Web applications, database software, servers, and complex security architectures. In some instances, the public's increased use of government Web services can require a doubling of infrastructure for a popular application. No longer can a useful internal business application be simply moved to a server outside the firewall and used by the public. Even after considering the quantifiable benefits of government Web services, the cost of providing secure and dependable interactive applications such as GIS is rising and requires specific budgeting.

Several local governments have divided their GIS Web-based services into two categories: public and subscription. In the public Web site, citizens have access to commonly requested datasets such as parcels, political boundaries, hydrology, contours, and land-use zoning. The public GIS application allows users to perform basic map functions and query capabilities. The subscription service is a pay-for-use system, either

Allen County, Indiana, and GIS external subscription services

What will be the outcome of fee-based GIS external subscription services? Allen County is one of the first local governments to test this option.

Allen County spent several years studying the feasibility of GIS technology and how to pay for it before taking the plunge in 1998. Once the GIS program got started and the database was constructed, the county's management faced the question of how to fund an enterprise-level GIS and provide external services.

Working with a consultant, the county conducted a market survey to assess the needs, benefits, and costs of the service. The estimated cost was $3.3 million over five years. Given the large number of services a GIS could potentially support, the Allen County Council decided that GIS should be self-funded as much as possible.

The county launched a program called iMap, a software system and business plan, with the intent to provide reliable and easy-to-access external services. While the project was not designed to be fully self-supporting,

Allen County, Indiana, and GIS external subscription services (cont.)

it did seek to recover 25 percent of the total GIS costs, including hardware, software, database development, and support. This cost-recovery goal played a significant role in the council's decision to approve the project. Revenue is generated through subscriptions and data purchases, offsetting part of the burden on the county's general fund.

The first external service was map plotting. Engineers, surveyors, and planners purchased prints of orthophotography and contours for use in preliminary land development projects. Alex Wernher, iMap system administrator, was surprised to find the demand for this service far exceeded expectations. Supporting the project requires 80 percent of one employee's time.

Selling digital data was the second revenue-generating service. Orthophotography and parcel datasets were the top sellers. The data was sold by section or as a countywide dataset. In 2004, the map plotting and data sale revenues were 20 percent higher than projected.

The next phase of the iMap program will be e-commerce GIS subscription services. The plan is to provide the public with a free GIS data viewer on the Internet. The viewer would contain all the data funded by public bond monies, such as the parcel data, with addresses, values, taxes, and home exemption attribution.

Several iMap subscription options would provide access to the full GIS database as well as advanced specialized query tools tailored to the needs of specific types of businesses such as real estate. Subscribers would choose from various levels of service:
- A single user requesting all data associated with a parcel would be charged $1 per parcel.
- A company could query an unlimited number of parcels for $40 per month per user.
- A corporation with four daily users would pay a quarterly fee of $400.
- A city or other public agency could subscribe to the entire database, paying between $0.40 and $1.25 per parcel depending on their use and interest.

The map plotting, digital data, and subscription services are all presented on a single Web page interface, which helps users learn about the different offerings.

Allen County realizes many benefits from external services beyond the revenue generated, Wernher said, "As more people use the GIS data, users are finding database errors and discrepancies that are fixed, which improves the quality and integrity of the database." Local engineers and surveyors have expanded their services and become more self-sufficient due to the mapping provided by Allen County. For example, the Indiana Department of Transportation (IDOT) worked on a flood mitigation project using ten-foot contours. A local surveyor used Allen County's two-foot contours to quickly develop three alternative plans. The IDOT accepted the better data, reducing the project's cost to the community by half. And as the subscription services become available, the assessor/treasurer's office should see significant savings on staff time spent on tasks such as faxing records to real estate companies.

When Allen County began the iMap program, it conducted a local and national survey of GIS users, asking about data use and services. Thirty-six local engineering firms and title companies, and 250 members of Urban and Regional Information System Association (URISA) completed the survey. The results indicated that there would be a high demand for data. The national survey also showed that 74 percent of the agencies do not charge for data distribution. Indiana statues allow jurisdictions to charge for enhanced data access, which is not the case in many other states. Allen County is one of the first to implement fee-based external services. Local government leaders across the country look forward to seeing the results.

Based on an interview with Alex Wernher, iMap system administrator for Allen County.

a one-time charge for a query or a subscription fee for yearly unlimited viewing. The subscription service provides access to many more datasets, and software functionality includes property analysis and advanced searches.

As local government GIS Web services grow in number and complexity, local governments will need to decide if current budget levels can sustain this growth or if subscription services should partially or fully fund these useful e-government services.

Regional GIS services

Regional GIS describes a multijurisdictional GIS implementation. One agency hosts the GIS and provides services to subscribing partners. Such was the case with Pierce County's GIS, described in the in-depth case study accompanying this chapter. Alternatively, several agencies might partner together, sharing the cost and development of one GIS (eCityGov Alliance in chapter 2). Such partnerships involve sharing costs and decision making. This section explores the rationale and benefits of regional GIS, and provides guidelines for implementing a regional GIS as an external service.

If a local government GIS has complete and well-maintained datasets, customized applications, and the ability to support remote users from central servers, then it might want to expand the system to include external, subscribing agencies. In the subscriber business model, the subscribing partners use the same tools and systems in place on the existing host system. Subscribers pay for a proportional share of the hardware, software, system maintenance, and user support costs.

The rationale for participating in a regional GIS with subscribing partners includes the following:

- New database construction is costly. Sharing database development among partners reduces each partner's costs.
- Data sharing reduces data redundancy and the expense of maintaining multiple copies of the same data.
- Each partner benefits by having access to the other partners' datasets, which greatly expands the data available.
- Agencies that perform similar functions (for example, local government, fire districts, law enforcement) can share GIS applications. An application developed once can be used multiple times.
- GIS software and hardware support is costly. The cost for each partner is reduced by combining their resources.
- Internet technology and communication systems have matured to the point that regional GIS is possible and easy to implement.

A regional GIS with subscribing partners benefits both the subscribers and the hosting agency. Subscribers benefit from the service because they do not need to maintain the hardware and software. The GIS system itself provides the core business functions while the regional host maintains the data needed for base mapping. This allows subscribers to focus on creating specialized datasets and performing analysis on the host's existing platform. Subscribers can concentrate on using a GIS to answer questions rather than supporting and maintaining the GIS. The hosting agency benefits by using its existing system to expand its user base, increase the quantity and quality of its GIS data, and generate revenue.

Offering regional GIS services and access to large geographic data stores is easier than ever. Increasing GIS functionality available on the Internet allows an agency to build a robust Internet application and provide subscription services to other organizations. With Web-based regional services, the subscribing agency does not need to be local. If the application has an easy interface for uploading datasets to the central server, the server can be located anywhere. Transaction management and direct editing of GIS data layers is still maturing on the Web, which might limit subscribers' ability to maintain their data. If the goal is data viewing and analysis, however, a Web-based, regional GIS would be successful.

A negative side to a regional GIS service is the subscribers' dependence on the host GIS. Network problems and technical difficulties frustrate subscribers. Before subscribing to a regional GIS service, the subscribing agency should verify the host's system uptime and dependability.

External services provide ways for local governments to expand GIS use, improve their GIS database, and share costs. There is no standard price structure for GIS subscriptions. The rate should be based on the functionality of the system and a prorated share of the hardware, software, and support costs. The contracting terms for a regional GIS service should address network security (since subscribers are directly connecting to the host's network), how outages will be handled, and specific services. A sample subscription agreement contract is provided at the end of this book.

Licensing or transfer of software

A logical extension of the regional GIS concept is the licensing or transfer of GIS software from the agency developing the software to a user, which could be a commercial company or another jurisdiction. In a regional GIS business model, the GIS is hosted by one agency and others subscribe. Licensing or transfer of software involves one agency supplying software to another. The topic is included in this chapter because many agencies providing innovative e-government or regional services will be asked if their software can be shared with others.

The licensing or transfer of government-created software can spark a long discussion about government's role and ability to collect revenue and fees. Each jurisdiction may have local laws allowing or restricting the sale and distribution of government-created products. The intent of this section is not to recommend or discourage the practice, but to provide examples and guidelines. A sample product license agreement for software distribution is provided at the end of this book.

Licensing a jurisdiction's software allows the jurisdiction to retain ownership of the product while distributing it for others to use. The agency purchasing a license uses the software on its computer system and pays a fee for the use. The agency benefits from the immediate usability of the application, which can help speed a project along or quickly automate a business function. The downside is support for the product provided by the agency that developed it. Assuming the developer agency is also a user of the product, most bugs or software malfunctions should be minimal. Fixing problems would be at the discretion of the developer.

Transferring a jurisdiction's software involves a reassignment of ownership. The jurisdiction can continue to use the system, but no longer owns the software. This arrangement can be useful if the product has a commercial value or if there could be a third-party liability issue associated with the software's use. This was the case for Pierce County's Responder System (see the accompanying case study later in this chapter). The software system is used by law enforcement and fire protection services when responding to a school safety incident. Because many jurisdictions wanted to use the system and third-party tort claims could result, the county opted to transfer the software to a commercial software vendor for distribution.

The goal for most software licensing or transfer business models is generating revenue. In the licensing model, a per-user fee or an agency fee can be established. In the transfer model, a transfer fee can consist of a lump sum payment and royalties on future sales of the product. Generally the revenues are used to maintain or support the use of GIS in the jurisdiction.

Digital data services

Responding to requests for GIS data requires some basic, upfront decisions. Should GIS data distribution generate revenue or not? The actual method of supplying data is relatively simple once the goal of the GIS data program is determined. Many jurisdictions already made this decision as a result of laws allowing government agencies to charge a fee for database extracts (Croswell 2004). In other jurisdictions, open public records law has interpreted digital data requests to be the same as paper documents, and the only fee that can be charged is the cost of making a copy.

Why is this such a hot topic in the GIS industry? Under pressure to fund expensive GIS data conversion projects and maintenance, many local governments look to revenues from data distribution. The justification is that the data has commercial value (because requestors want it for projects), and the cost to develop, quality control, maintain, and disseminate the data should be included in the distribution fee. In this manner, taxpayers are not totally funding the GIS database. Given the constant pressure on general fund resources, local governments often look to a GIS to help recover a portion of its operating expenses, and digital data requests can be a revenue source if legislation is in place.

> In Allen County, Indiana, local leaders expected data sales and services to fully fund the GIS. Today the goal is to fund 25 percent of the budget

Others insist that GIS data should be provided at no charge or only for the cost of duplication. They argue that taxpayers have already paid to develop the data so it should be free and available to all for the public good. Taxpayers would benefit from the free data because competitive pressure will require the users of the data to correspondingly reduce the cost of their services to the public. A particular data request might be for studying an issue of public concern, or it might be for construction planning. These are investments in the community, aided by publicly available GIS data, which can promote a positive impression of government service.

> In Pierce County, Washington, requestors pay for the time to prepare the data. In the last two years, 270 data requests have been processed. Requestors included
> - forty engineering companies
> - four transit companies
> - five nonprofit organizations
> - ten school/colleges
> - fifteen other government agencies

> More colleges and universities now offer GIS classes and certificate programs as a result of the increase in local users of GIS. This in turn provides a resource for interns for the county's GIS.

A remaining question in the data request pay-or-not-to-pay discussion is how does this situation change if the data is value added or improved beyond what is required for government use? Should government agencies improve their data if the cost of doing so can be offset with revenue for the service? For example, most cities and counties have a street centerline dataset attributed with address ranges. This dataset may also have a transit route system built into it. What if the agency added street direction and turn information to this dataset, which would be useful for commercial purposes? Should the agency be able to charge for this value-added service? This scenario is similar to the Canadian and European model for cadastral data. The data is highly accurate, well maintained, and sold at what some consider a high price. But could the high quality be maintained without the sales revenue? The United States does not have a comparable national GIS dataset.

Perhaps in the future, a choice will need to be made between either increasing taxes or nationalizing data sales in order to develop and maintain a high-quality infrastructure for GIS.

Managing a GIS data request service

A government GIS agency can run an effective GIS data request service that minimizes the staff time required, recovers costs, and most importantly, encourages the use of GIS data in the community. After deciding on fees for data services, the next step is to reach consensus among data custodians (departments that create and maintain GIS data files) on how to authorize the release of data. If the GIS data is the responsibility of one group, then this group can decide how to review requests and authorize releases. If multiple departments are responsible for GIS data, it can be efficient to appoint one group to coordinate responses to data requests. This group can forward a request for approval by the specific department that owns the data and knows of any governing laws that may restrict the release of data. Once approved, the coordinator can prepare the data for release and maintain a record of the request.

The various methods to provide GIS digital data services include direct download CD production, and custom data requests.

Method: Direct download of files

Description	Many local governments do not have the resources to respond individually to each data request. GIS data files are loaded onto an FTP site or Web site with instructions on how to access and download the data files. The data files are periodically updated.
Cost	Jurisdiction has the minimal cost of maintaining the FTP or Web site.
Pros	Minimizes staff time to support digital data requests. No need for department to approve data request.
Cons	It is difficult to enforce restrictions on the commercial use of lists if the people downloading data are unknown. The online data may not be the most current version unless the jurisdiction updates the online site after data maintenance.

Method: Produce a CD of datasets

Description	Data files and metadata are copied onto a CD for distribution. Often jurisdictions prepare a set of CDs quarterly or annually. A master CD is created and then duplicated by a vendor.
Cost	Jurisdictions typically charge for the production of the CD plus any data costs.
Pros	Creating the master CD requires staff time, but then distribution is very simple—just mailing a CD. Data use can be monitored because the requestor is known.
Cons	The data on CD is not the most current version. Depending on the frequency of updating the master CD and producing copies, the data can be very outdated. It can be difficult to estimate how many CDs to create. If too many are made, the surplus represents a lost expense for the jurisdiction.

Method: Custom data requests

Description	Data requests are prepared at the time of request. Based on the project needs of the requestor, data files, and metadata are copied onto a CD or to an FTP site for distribution.
Cost	Typically, the cost to the requestor is the hourly rate for staff to prepare the data files (about one to three hours) plus any data fees.
Pros	Data requests can be evaluated to ensure they comply with the public records law. Requestors speak to GIS staff members who can help them evaluate which data files might be best for the project.
Cons	Requires staff dedicated to responding to each data request in a timely manner.

Servicing GIS data requests can be a way to expand the use and benefits of a GIS. As with any set of procedures, there are always exceptions to general rules, and determining how to respond to these will ensure an equitable standard. Exceptions often include the following:

Universities and educational institutions

A useful dataset can be prepared once a year and supplied to any educational group at no cost.

Students Local community colleges and universities with GIS programs may require students to complete a GIS project as part of their studies. Students do not want to pay for data, so local governments can provide a standard educational dataset or refer them to a university that has a copy of the dataset.

Newspapers and media

The media generally have little to no budget for data, but want the most current data and question paying for it. Local governments can provide them with the educational dataset and request they pay for any custom service.

Consultants/contractors for jurisdiction

Jurisdictions hiring consultants, engineers, or contractors for projects may provide GIS data files to them at no cost as it will help complete work more quickly.

Nonprofit organizations

Nonprofit organizations may request data for environmental studies or demographic analysis. Most nonprofits do not have funds to pay for the data, and most jurisdictions provide the data at no charge to these groups.

Other government agencies

Peer agencies or state agencies may request data at no cost and offer to share data in exchange. These requests should be individually evaluated to determine if the data exchange is useful and equitable.

Commercial mapping companies

Commercial mapping or GIS companies may request GIS data as a base data layer for their own system or to incorporate into a commercial product. Generally, these companies request street centerline and address data for geocoding. These requests can be yearly or more frequently and should be charged at the standard data request rate.

GIS data disclaimers are included in digital data requests to protect against litigation. The terms and conditions stipulate the proper use, conditions, exceptions, and liability of using the data files. Sample GIS data disclaimers are provided at the back of this book. A helpful restriction (although difficult to enforce) is not allowing requestors to secondarily disseminate the jurisdiction's GIS data. Without including a specific restriction on the secondary dissemination of data, the requestor could provide the jurisdiction's data to others without any disclaimers. If the data was misused or caused harm, the jurisdiction could potentially be at risk. This restriction can be justified by reminding requestors that everyone should contact the jurisdiction to ensure they are getting the most current and accurate GIS data.

Data requests can help a jurisdiction build a larger GIS database by asking data requestors to supply their project data results (if nonproprietary) back to the jurisdiction. If data requestors use the data to perform a spatial analysis, map environmental conditions, or prepare a new subdivision plat, their project files can add useful data back to the GIS.

Public requests for digital data can be an important part of a local government's GIS external services, but responding to these requests require staff time and good customer service skills. By implementing defendable policies and procedures for digital data requests, staff time, and some costs can be reduced. New data can be added to the GIS, and when requestors report data errors, the datasets can be corrected. A good digital data request program can lead to positive results and a valuable GIS external service.

Mapping, consulting, and training services

If a local government has implemented a GIS, it also has probably received external requests for creating custom maps, discussing GIS implementation, or providing GIS training. Such services may be among those provided to other departments within the local government. Depending on how the GIS budget is structured, a fee may or may not be charged for the services. If the services are already being provided internally, offering them to external clients for a fee should be explored.

The business case for mapping, consulting, and training services is very similar to that described in the previous section on a regional GIS service. For local governments that have GIS staff with the skills, expertise, procedures, and materials already prepared for internal clients, very little extra work is needed to expand services to external clients. Requests for these services can come from agencies with less GIS experience, the public, nonprofit organizations, school districts, and transportation agencies. The services can be individually priced based on an hourly rate for the GIS staff and the time needed.

Offering these services externally may seem like a simple step and an opportunity to create new revenue, but there are two important factors to consider:

1. An increasing number of civil engineering and environmental consulting companies are becoming knowledgeable about GIS, and many offer mapping, consulting, data analysis, and training services. A local government must consider whether its GIS services would compete or conflict with local businesses. If local government wants to attract such firms as part of its economic development goals, it may be better to use local firms rather than compete with them. An exception to this may be a request for service that requires knowledge of specific GIS data or the unique expertise of the local government's GIS staff.

2. Services such as creating custom maps, consulting, and training require an individual to perform the service. With a custom service, there is little opportunity to reuse the product for a second client that would create an economy of scale. For example, a software developer writes a script that performs an analysis and generates a report. The script can be sold to multiple clients with no additional labor. Services such as custom map production, consulting, and training cannot be sold to a second client without additional direct labor. This is important to consider because most GIS staff members already have a full schedule supporting clients. Adding clients and services may not be possible.

If a local government determines its GIS team has unique skills and can find the time to support new clients and generate new revenue, it might consider providing these services:

Mapping services

Custom maps are comprised of specific data layers for a geographic area. Custom text placement, symbology, and cartography are required. Projects can involve producing one map or creating an entire map atlas.

Data analysis services can include a specific spatial analysis project and a map created for the client. This could include demographic, environmental, or land-use analysis. The resulting map product could include one or more maps to describe the analysis process.

Consulting services

Data consulting services can include developing data conversion specifications, preparing requests for proposals for data conversion, and designing quality control and quality assurance practices during data conversion.

Another service might include offering database design and data modeling consulting for complex data systems, such as cadastral/parcel databases, road centerline/route databases, and zoning/land-use databases that may also require a historical component.

Start-up services for organizations acquiring GIS is a popular offering. Services could include consulting on hardware, software, database development, project implementation, and GIS organizational issues.

Specialty consulting services assist on a particular task or project. This can include performing data collection with GPS equipment, creating a route system on a road centerline file, or performing data quality control for a new database. The service is based on a needed skill or the ability to provide the needed resources within the schedule to complete the project.

Software development

Software services include developing scripts, software applications, software functionality, or Web sites. For local governments that have GIS staff with specialized knowledge of a GIS database, it may be more cost effective for a client to request this work be performed by that staff.

Training

Specialized classes on GIS applications, analysis, and data can be a useful service. Many large GIS organizations have a training program in which external agencies can purchase training at a reasonable rate.

Mapping, consulting, and training services offer opportunities to generate revenue for GIS organizations and to expand GIS use and expertise in the community. These external services can help build partnerships with other organizations, which can lead to new GIS subscriptions.

Web application services

A new breed of external services is emerging. Web application services are Web-based software functions (such as geocoding) or custom software applications that use generic datasets. As nationwide datasets are created and jurisdictions contribute to framework initiatives for cadastral, transportation, and image framework databases, generic Web applications can be created to use these datasets. Local governments are uniquely positioned to develop and host Web application services because they serve as custodians for large datasets and have already constructed business systems that use the data.

There are opportunities for many local governments to design and host Web applications, which can then be used by other jurisdictions for a subscription fee. For example, a Web application to geographically search for sex offenders in a neighborhood would be useful for any jurisdiction. This application uses a street center-line and address data file and a geocoded sex offender dataset. The application might be hosted by the developing agency for a yearly fee that includes hardware, software, and system administration. This benefits the developer agency by generating revenue from existing applications and benefits the subscribing agency by saving the time and cost to develop and maintain the application. This approach, if carried to the extreme, would allow local government GIS users to develop state-of-the-art uses for GIS and share the results. For example, perhaps jurisdiction A develops an excellent pavement management system, and jurisdiction B develops a superior parcel management system. By subscribing to each other's applications, these jurisdictions are able to implement excellent GIS applications quickly and cheaply.

Jurisdictions interested in creating and hosting GIS Web services may not have enough surplus server capacity to accommodate subscribing agencies. This problem can be solved by using an application service provider (ASP) to host the application on a server farm. The ASP's charges are typically based on usage the application receives. The costs are much lower than purchasing the hardware and upgraded bandwidth needed to provide the same level of computing capacity. Also, server maintenance and support are included in the ASP services.

Web application services can be viewed as a natural extension of a regional GIS service where agencies come together to share applications. With Web application services, however, the agencies do not need to be geographically close to each other. Good Web service development uses flexible architecture, nonprocedural design, object-oriented-modular software, and tools for data upload and administration. This will allow the Web service to be useful for the largest number of people with diverse datasets. For example, a Web service might be developed that locates an address and finds all user-specified features within a distance of the address, displays a map of the search, and reports the results. This Web service could be used to find area parks or dentists or recycling centers or eagle nests within a certain distance from a specific address. In each case, the functionality of the Web service is the same. Only the data changes to meet a particular need.

Web application services are a new opportunity for local governments to enhance their custom GIS business applications and provide new external services. For a hosting agency, software development and maintenance costs are shared with subscribers. For a subscribing agency, new applications can be deployed quickly and without in-house development and maintenance costs. Through the use of Web services, the participating organizations benefit by mutually sharing their individual strengths, making it easier to implement better applications quickly with less effort and cost, and dramatically improving the cost-benefit ratio for the whole GIS community.

Conclusions

Implementing and managing an enterprise GIS is a complex and time-consuming task of meeting user expectations, ensuring data quality and accuracy, creating new uses for the technology, and communicating results regularly.

External services are a natural extension of traditional GIS. Internal business applications to view parcel information or zoning criteria can be leveraged fairly quickly into an external service. It should not take much time to implement external services, using the existing expertise of the GIS staff. It greatly expands a local government's ability to provide public service, fosters multijurisdictional partnerships, lowers data development costs, and increases the use of GIS technology in a region. And, in some instances, external services can also provide additional revenue for a GIS budget. Consider carefully the opportunities and business case for each potential external service, and determine the types of service that will enhance a local government GIS.

Pierce County, Washington

Profile—County government	
Location	West Central Washington
Size (miles square)	1,025 square miles
Population	700,000
Form of government	County council-executive
Annual GIS operating budget	$2.5 million
Employees in GIS unit	17 FTEs, plus "super users" in larger county departments
Governmental departments using GIS	25

Overview

Pierce County, in west central Washington, has a very robust and well-established GIS program. The county provides numerous GIS-based Web services to county residents, and continues to develop new GIS applications and application enhancements. This case study describes the evolution of external GIS services in the county and highlights some of the more innovative examples of such services.

Background

Pierce County's planning and land services department spearheaded the effort to bring GIS to the county in 1989. At the time, a new statewide mandate on growth management required extensive land-use analysis. The planning department felt a countywide GIS would help meet the terms of the mandate by improving the county's ability to produce maps and alternative plans, and facilitate communication with the public. Planning department staff began demonstrating the new technology and talked to other departments about how a centralized system would eliminate duplicate mapping efforts.

In 1990, the county introduced its first GIS application, a redistricting program for the county auditor's office. The application used U.S. Census Bureau's TIGER/Line data to capture street centerline and address information, and U.S. Census population data to analyze population shifts within the county. The new application made it possible for the county to quickly produce new precinct maps and institute the redistricting based on population changes. Linda Gerull, GIS manager for Pierce County, said the choice of developing this particular application was a matter of what would benefit the most users. "This dataset enabled the maximum number of users to begin using the GIS," she said.

Building support for the system meant winning over the county's political leadership and managers. Presentations to county council members showcased the larger problem-solving capabilities of a GIS, while presentations to department directors and managers centered on the potential business applications and how daily work assignments could be completed more quickly and accurately.

In 1992, the county council contracted with a consultant to produce a feasibility study for significantly expanding the GIS program. The study focused on the most cost-effective expansion, looking at needs, potential uses, costs, and expected benefits. In weighing the costs against the anticipated benefits, the study suggested that it would take about seven years for the expansion to pay for itself. Based on the study's findings, the county council committed $2 million to begin database development for building an enterprise GIS.

One of the main reasons for creating the system was to consolidate information within the county. At the time, the county had more than eighteen different street maps and address databases, and none of them matched each other. Through consolidation, a single source of information was maintained and distributed for use by the whole county government. This move also enabled the county to greatly increase the accuracy of the information and provide more timely data with fewer errors.

According to Steven Bailey, director of the Department of Emergency Management, the GIS had a visionary beginning with a basic system that would facilitate many different programs. "And, most importantly, the GIS program administrators were willing to sit down and explore the unknown of where GIS could go," he said. "They were very receptive to questions and new ideas. . .. I commend them for that because it created a culture of innovation."

Organizational issues

One of the chief concerns at the outset of expanding the GIS was providing access for all county departments. Like all county government, Pierce County's departments come in "all different sizes," said Terry Hale, director of the Department of Information Services (IS). Some—like the assessor/treasurer, planning and land services, and public works—are very large, while others are very small. All are important, but GIS staff time is limited and every department cannot get equal attention.

County managers tackled this issue on a number of fronts. First, they located the GIS team as a division within the IS department, where it was treated as an internal service for all county departments. This location helped create an important synergy because the GIS team receives support from the other divisions within IS. For example, the Production Services Division and PC and Network Division handled all hardware and network support services for the county. That enabled the GIS team to focus exclusively on developing and enhancing GIS tools.

For the larger departments, county management helped identify staff members who could serve as super users. Super users function as in-house GIS experts, coordinating GIS activities within a department and serving as a resource for other users. The GIS team provides the super users with additional training and support to ensure the departments have sufficient in-house expertise to build databases and use GIS.

Also, the GIS team developed a desktop Web-based application called CountyView, which provides easy access to the county's ever-growing GIS database. CountyView gives users a fully-powered GIS application

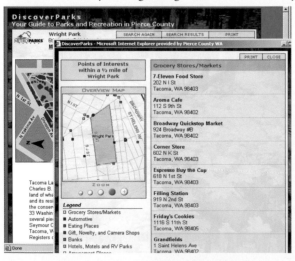

Figure 5.3 Pierce County's parks Web sites uses GIS technology to help residents locate nearby parks by address, ZIP code, or city or search for a park based on facilities needed.

Source: Pierce County, Wash.

with tools for tapping more than six hundred county-maintained datasets. The central database avoids data duplication throughout county government.

External services

Pierce County has provided GIS data to the public since 1997 and has had public Internet GIS applications available since 1998. The county offers numerous GIS-based Web services to county residents with more under development each year. Among the online GIS services available to the public are

- **CensusView 2000.** Allows users to view and search for various census data about Pierce County.
- **Discover Parks.** Permits searches for spatial information on county parks and their facilities.
- **Geodata Express.** Facilitates online ordering of GIS data.
- **Info by Address-Auditor.** Enables an address query by precinct for voter information
- **Info by Address-Council.** Enables an address query for elected official information.
- **Map Gallery.** Lets users access, download, and print official county maps.
- **Map-Your-Way.** Functions as an interactive GIS with query tools, map displays, and data reporting.
- **Neighborhood Crime.** Lets users query current crime statistics and trends by neighborhood.
- **Parcel Search.** Provides access to land parcel details and maps.
- **Property Sales Comparables Search.** Provides geographical search tools for property sales comparables, based on various characteristics.
- **First Source.** Allows users to look for human resources by address.
- **Sex Offender Registry.** Helps users look up sex offender information by address and neighborhood location.
- **Survey Control and Monument.** Enables users to look up, view, and map survey monuments.

Gerull said the county's most popular public Web sites, such as the Parcel Search and Map-Your-Way, provide different types of land-use information. Users of these sites can pull up county maps and then drill down to information about specific properties. The Property Sales Comparables Search site, which answers real estate value questions, is expected to attract a tremendous amount of traffic in years to come, she said.

The county also provides online GIS services to local agencies throughout the region. Cities, the health department, private businesses, and fire agencies take advantage of the county's GIS to share the cost for technology each could not otherwise afford. Ten agencies throughout the region subscribe to the county's regional GIS. All subscribers receive online access to the GIS, data storage space, training for up to eight users, and ten hours of technical support each month. By using one system, the size and value of the GIS database expands, improving the overall quality and accuracy. By partnering on data construction projects, the county and subscribers lower their cost to build new datasets.

Providing these services involves a slight increase in the overall budget for the GIS. Some of the cost is offset by the yearly subscription fees from the online subscribers, approximately $180,000 each year. Small GPS data-collection projects that county staff conducts for subscribing agencies is a secondary revenue stream. Subscribers leverage the expertise of the county's GIS staff and equipment, building drainage inventories and fire hydrant inventories.

With several successful Web-based GIS applications, the county encourages other jurisdictions to use them. With Web technology, an application can reside anywhere and still be maintained by Pierce County, which keeps costs low and support easy. The sex offender registry Web site and the corresponding sex offender verification system are used by several other jurisdictions. These jurisdictions were attracted to

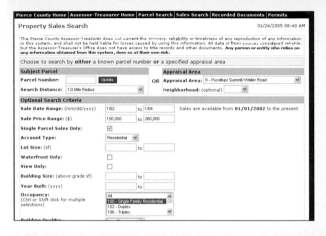

a.

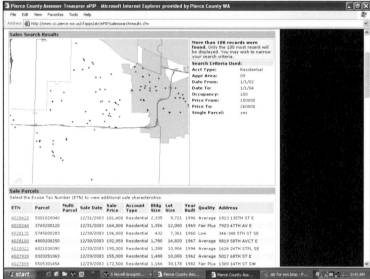

b.

Figures 5.4a and b Pierce County's electronic Property Information Profile (e-PIP) allows individuals to compare their property to property sales in the area. This function is particularly popular for people looking to buy or sell property or evaluate their tax appraisal.

Source: Pierce County, Wash.

Web-based GIS because applications are low-cost and can be online quickly, avoiding time-consuming software development.

The county has also been able to sell its GIS applications as products to commercial businesses. The county transfers ownership of the application to the vendor and receives royalties whenever another jurisdiction implements the application.

Public information and community engagement

Beyond providing new services to county residents, the GIS program has helped the county government engage the public in its work. Bailey said the uniqueness of some of the county's GIS applications, particularly those

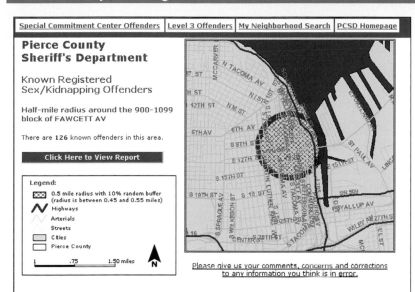

Figure 5.5 Pierce County's online registry of sex and kidnapping offenders provides its citizens with information about the location of offenders living in the community, helping to increase personal safety through increased awareness.

Source: Pierce County, Wash.

developed for the department of emergency management, has generated a lot of local publicity. "It affords us the opportunity to tell the story of how we are using technology to ensure public safety," he said.

Bailey's staff and the GIS team developed two such applications, the Crisis Communications Web site and the Pierce County Neighborhood Action Team Program. The Crisis Communications site, created in 1998, takes over the county's main Web site during an emergency and provides specific information about the current event. The site contains maps, guidelines for the public, and background information for the media. During Puget Sound's Nisqually Earthquake of 2001, the Crisis Communications Web site proved invaluable for letting residents look up where damage had occurred in the county, which highways and roads were passable, and where people could receive assistance.

The Pierce County Neighborhood Action Team Program helps train neighborhood groups to sustain themselves for up to seventy-two hours after an emergency. These groups are trained in emergency response, first aid, and communication in the event of a disaster. They can be eyes and ears in the field, providing up-to-date information for the county. The GIS maps the location of these groups and ties the mapping to an in-depth database about each group's participants, training, and contact information. During an emergency, news from the neighborhood teams helps generate preliminary damage assessments around the county.

Land development is another area the county has used to garner considerable public involvement through its GIS program. Proposed plans for the Chambers Creek Properties, an old gravel pit on the Puget Sound coast, call for the county to build a championship golf course on the site. The GIS team helped develop a Web site for the public to view the most recent plans and proposals for the property. A comment feature on the Web site allows residents to provide feedback on the plan without having to attend public meetings.

Changing relationships

Providing external GIS services has changed the nature of the county's relationship with its residents, local businesses, academic institutions, and other organizations. GIS technology allows government to present information in a much more useable way for citizens who no longer have to sift through reports and printouts of data, Hale said. "Many of the external services the county offers are totally new public services. By providing new and innovative services, citizens see government as being responsive and helpful. The feedback we receive from citizens and businesses shows us that we are definitely providing the information and tools needed," he said.

For example, engineering and survey firms in the county take advantage of the digital data available through the GIS and the Survey Web site. Because the firms have direct access to the data and do not have to use staff time tracking it down from a variety of sources, they are able to reduce project costs and schedules. As a result, the firms are more competitive.

Once these private firms started using the county's GIS data routinely, a demand for GIS training in the region developed. The area's community colleges responded by offering GIS certificate programs. As people graduate from these programs, the demand for GIS data from the county has continued to increase. The growing number of GIS users working with local data has made a greater base of community support for the county's GIS program.

"GIS has become the focal point for building relationships, and brought in groups that normally would not be in a room together," said Bailey. In other words, developing new GIS applications provides a reason for different groups to establish working relationships that improve efficiency.

Future services

Bailey hopes to see the county's GIS become even more interactive in the future. He wants to give county residents an opportunity to provide information, not just be the recipients of it. On homeland security issues in particular, he would like to provide a way for residents to alert the county about potential problems they might see.

Hale and Gerull point to the increasing number of regulations imposed by state and federal governments as a driver of new GIS applications. For example, citizens need to understand new state environmental regulations that impact county development plans. The GIS team conducted several data analyses of the new restrictions and developed a Web site to make these analyses available to the public. Citizens can review environmental conditions before applying for a permit. Frequently, residents come to the county offices to get a permit, but often they do not know nor understand what they need to bring. This new Web site helps people prepare, so there will not be as many surprises. It also helps them understand the need for the permit based on environmental conditions in their neighborhood.

Business reasons for inventing new services for citizens pop up every year. Hale said, "Current technology allows us to provide these services very economically to the community and public service is improved. We keep amazing ourselves."

Advice to other local governments

Hale and Gerull agreed that other local governments should take time to develop a culture that supports GIS. To build such a culture requires listening to the needs of all the departments, big and small, and then working in partnership to develop applications that fulfill those needs. Hale maintained that if GIS users work together, they can build databases that support the entire organization, not just one department or program. "The real value is when all the departments share their data," he said. "It's such an eye-opener, because they learn that GIS complements all."

References

Croswell, Peter. 2004. Legal and policy issues impacting public agency GIS data and product distribution and sale. Presentation at the 2004 Georgia URISA GIS Conference.

GAO (General Accounting Office). 2003. Geographic information systems: Challenges to effective data sharing. Document no. GAO-03-874T. Washington, D.C.: General Accounting Office.

6

Emerging issues, trends, and technologies

Patrick J. Bresnahan, PhD
Geographic Information Officer, Richland County, South Carolina

GIS implementation is inevitable

Does anyone think about using applied radioactivity in the home to rapidly cook food? Probably not. But it was only a few decades ago when the microwave oven was new and somewhat intimidating. Could grandpa and his pacemaker remain in the room while the microwave was on? Today, the microwave oven is as common as the refrigerator in household kitchens. No longer acknowledged for its application of radioactive elements, its use is ubiquitous. The microwave oven has become part of everyday life.

This volume focuses on implementing and applying GIS in local government, where this technology is also becoming a part of everyday life. GIS has had a place in larger governments and academic institutions for more than forty years, but only recently has it become commonplace in city and county operations. And it will continue to evolve as it is leveraged in small businesses as well as personal information and location devices. Implementing GIS and related technologies in local government still requires a champion to sell the real and practical benefits. However, as GIS becomes more widespread, it will have to be implemented at all levels of government. Local government managers must be prepared to manage this technology as service delivery becomes dependent upon it. This chapter provides a brief look at the technologies and issues related to this emerging infrastructure changing the business of local governing.

Introduction

Unlike many technological advances used by local government operations, GIS can unify personnel, information resources, and decision-making functions. Through a GIS, thematic data and applications can save time, lives, and money while providing local government administrators and elected officials with a resource to improve governance. Observers can find examples of such efficiencies in local government operations across the country.

GIS-based pavement management programs in public works departments judiciously identify infrastructure needs while simultaneously supporting an inventory of assets for accounting requirements. Handheld GIS applications for mosquito control streamline paperwork and data entry while enabling a coordinated response to infectious disease events. This technology has permeated nearly every departmental function of local government. Administrators and managers must be prepared to leverage such opportunities and efficiencies to improve, and sometimes extend, public service delivery.

Almost all large local governments (populations greater than 100,000) employ GIS and related technologies, but it has not reached smaller communities to the same degree (PTI 2003). Funding barriers have limited GIS use in many smaller local governments. However, declining technology costs and evolving business practices will open a window of opportunity for these communities. More importantly, the environment in which local governments operate is changing rapidly, and such technology serves as a great equalizer by enabling small communities to compete in the global economy. Not only must such change be expected, it must also be managed.

The dynamic nature of technologies and business practices must be considered in planning and implementing any GIS. If these characteristics are not addressed, the system will be severely limited. System planning should allow for introducing new components whether they are hardware, software, data, analytical methods, or management practices. To do so requires diligence by all local users, to varying degrees. Furthermore, technological implementation is often the product of changing political or administrative priorities. Often, projects are initiated or redirected due to constituent feedback that, in turn, initiates action to address specific tasks or issues. Managers report to elected officials who, while detached from technical detail, often see the prospect of novel technology as an indication of progress. Efficiencies, then, must be exploited to manage core functions and tangential needs.

Keeping abreast of trends and evolving technologies is critical for maximizing the impact of GIS in local government management. The costs of falling behind in technology can be counted in both dollars and lives. GIS improves management of assets, resulting in hard dollar cost savings from accounting and budget perspectives. More importantly, geographic information is increasingly used in emergency response and routing, where saved seconds saves lives. Using real-time vehicle location data, the closest ambulance is dispatched to treat a heart attack victim. GIS road data can assure the most expeditious route for emergency vehicles to an incident location while accounting for impedances such as one-way streets, median barriers, and lane restrictions.

Just as there is a cost in falling behind, tangible benefits result from exploiting the cutting edge. For instance, evolving spatial database structures have made the storage and dissemination of immense image data archives more cost-effective and efficient. Advances in remote sensing, such as lidar (LIght Detection And Ranging) and aerial digital imaging, have reduced the cost of data collection while improving results. Improved storage and access to image data greatly benefit citizens and businesses by providing them with high-resolution aerial images that convey far greater detail about the land. Lower data costs of new technologies allow local governments to collect imagery more often. Thus, observable changes from development in the community can be reviewed by all citizens (*figures 6.1a and b*).

Other costs or savings come from adhering to outdated policies (costs) or adopting forward-looking ones (savings). For example, adhering to outdated standards that require the use of film-based aerial imagery and paper maps, as defined by state regulation, represents significant and unnecessary costs (SC 2004). On the other hand, significant savings come through updating local government practices such as instituting digital data submission for building permits (McGray 2001). Additionally, mandates from state and federal agencies require change, while incentive programs provide new opportunity. Thus, it remains difficult to achieve a balance between additional investments required for GIS implementation and tallying quantifiable results.

The underlying theme of this chapter is change—how GIS can help local governments manage change and how the GIS environment itself is changing. This chapter introduces managers to several key issues, trends,

a   b

Figures 6.1a and b   GIS helps communities better understand the effect of physical changes as development occurs.
These aerial images illustrate changes in land development in Richland County, South Carolina.

Source: Richland County, S.C.

and technologies that will affect local governments and their GIS programs in the coming years. These items
include the following:

- managing change in the community
  - service delivery
  - governance and public policy
  - public information and community engagement
- managing change in GIS technology
  - evolution of GIS in local government
  - GIS expertise
  - legal issues
  - standards
  - technologies

As with information in the preceding chapters, there is no correct manner in which to address these topics.
Simply considering them or formulating a strategy to address topics as they arise is a step toward success.

Managing change

GIS technology adoption has accelerated at a rate parallel to the introduction and improvement of personal
computing. When introduced, GIS was the domain of national and state governments as well as a few academic facilities, namely institutions with fairly significant budgets. Implemented in 1964, the Canada Geographic Information System (CGIS) moved spatial data analyses from manual methods to bits and bytes. That
national system was followed by the New York Landuse and Natural Resources Information System in 1967,
and the Minnesota Land Management Information System in 1969 (Star and Estes 1990). A survey in the
mid-1970s (Salem et al. 1977) compared capabilities of just fifty-four operational GIS, which were dominated
by federal, state, and university programs. The data structures and functionality associated with these systems
often focused on answering a very limited question set.

Commercial GIS began to grow with the availability of desktop computers in the 1980s. Constantly expanding computing power, together with GIS software designed for the desktop environment, fueled a surge in GIS

use from the late 1980s through 2000. Increasing capabilities in network computing, transferring large amounts of data via the Internet, and hardware portability have pushed the technology along in its latest growth phase. Such technological change has supported the expansion of GIS beyond its original governmental uses.

This history shows a distinct pattern of technological dissemination and absorption. GIS originated in federal programs that could afford to support costly proprietary systems. Those programs also included data at a resolution considered coarse in today's environment *(figure 6.2)*. In the 1970s and 1980s, GIS moved into state agencies and large corporations. Data was available at a finer resolution (thirty meters), and costs had lowered to the point where several agencies within a single state could support a GIS for a specific thematic mission *(figures 6.3a and b)*. During this period, features started to be represented by detailed linework instead of course grid cells, data collection costs declined, and new applications blossomed. In the 1990s, decreasing costs and an expanding set of applications helped GIS enter the local government domain. In recent years, the resolution of data collected and maintained by local governments has increased dramatically *(figures 6.4a and b)*. The trend in GIS use is continuing to the next level of users in small businesses and households, and at a higher resolution than ever before.

Since its beginning in the 1960s through today, the costs of GIS development have decreased while the resolution of the data has increased, making the technology more accessible and useful to all potential users. This trend will continue as GIS is adopted by all local governments and exploited in small businesses and personal use applications. Once the technology has been incorporated into all personal appliances or gadgetry, automated geography will be just another part of everyday life. People will no longer stop to think about GIS,

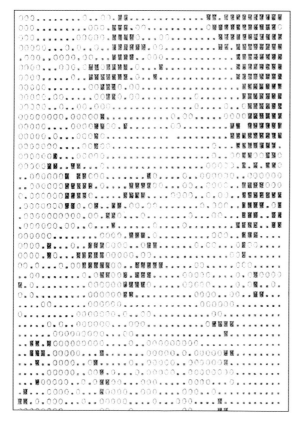

Figure 6.2 Data resolution in the 1970s is considered very coarse by today's standards. Here, land-cover data is shown at the resolution most commonly available in the 1970s.

Source: Richland County, S.C.

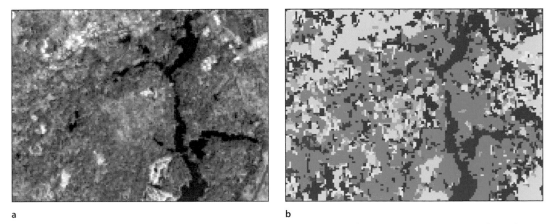

a   b

Figure 6.3a and b   GIS technology allows local governments to show the impact of a proposed development in relationship to community surroundings. This allows residents to have a much better sense of how the development will fit into their community.

Source: Richland County, S.C.

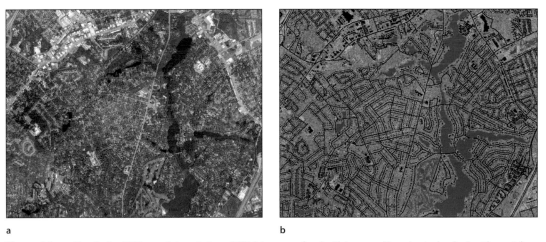

a   b

Figures 6.4a and b   By the 1990s, spatial resolution of GIS data were refined with improved imaging technologies. The aerial image presented here shows one-foot aerial imagery used for land-cover classification.

Source: Richland County, S.C.

GPS, or remote sensing technologies as they look at their watch to find the nearest hardware store where they can pick up the exact amount of fertilizer needed for the front yard.

Local governments collect the highest resolution, most accurate, and most up-to-date data available. The collective cost of this data runs in the billions of dollars. As local government is home to the official recording of most land changes, such as property division, street development, and land grading, among others, it has become the referential source for most geospatial data (Williamson et al. 2003). Understanding the trends of GIS adoption and absorption, local governments must be prepared to manage the responsibilities and opportunities of geospatial data as they become the guardians of the source data used by citizens and businesses as well as state and federal agencies.

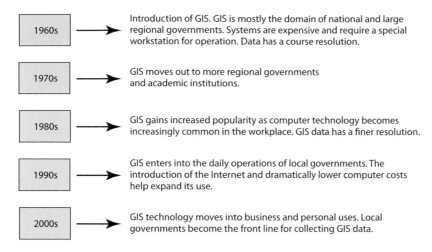

Figure 6.5 The evolution of GIS technology by decade.

Prepared by Patrick Bresnahan and Cory Fleming

Local government is the focus of the latest phase of GIS adoption in society. Change within local governments comes at a smaller scale but represents a diverse user base. Local government managers must address several types of change that play into plans for implementing GIS. These changes include

- service delivery
- governance and public policy
- public involvement and community engagement

Service delivery

One of the most valuable benefits of GIS is the ability to bring disparate information together in a common framework. Traditionally, local government departments such as public works, planning, zoning, and economic development have had limited interaction regarding service delivery and decision making. By organizing data from each department in a common spatial context, these departments have the capability to make decisions based on community-wide goals. For example, an enterprise GIS allows a land disturbance permit to be issued through the engineering department's evaluation of landcover and forest species information that planning personnel maintains. Ombudsman offices can also provide detailed information regarding government assets and activities during call-taking while simultaneously providing service departments specific locations for work-order management.

By implementing GIS as a framework for doing business in various departments, integrating information across service lines becomes practicable. The significance of this concept is borne of improved service delivery through evolving processes and procedures. While efficiencies are achieved in thematic department business, they are magnified when combined with other departments. Thus, doing business spatially opens the door for improved internal and external service delivery.

Furthermore, one of the most requested business applications in computer software is the ability to log the location of services within reports and records. Incident reports that include location determine jurisdiction and relevance; they also help to identify trends or potential hot spots within a community. Whether indicating the distance between a stop sign and an automobile accident or where a lost dog was picked up, location is growing more important in local governance. The analysis of such data allows local government to meet community needs while incorporating the results in the institutional business structure.

The in-depth case study accompanying this chapter showcases Honolulu's GIS, one of the most advanced local government GIS in the country. Public works employees use GPS receivers tied into the GIS to instantly track work history at a site. For example, employees can scan bar codes on manhole covers to determine when repair or maintenance was last done. Paper records and files are no longer needed to track work orders. The instantaneous nature of the technology allows the workers to quickly finish their jobs and move on to the next site, greatly enhancing employee productivity and improving service delivery.

Governance and public policy

GIS profoundly impacts governance and public policy. The technology clearly shows policy makers the different connections within a community and how their decisions will influence its development. Policy is often derived from reaction to individual situations or issues. With the information gathering and scenario building capabilities of GIS, managers and elected officials can evaluate community concerns as they develop. As local government managers are exposed to the benefits from coordinated and accessible geographic information, the local policy-making process can move away from being reactive in nature and closer to a proactive posture. For example, Miami-Dade County, Florida, used GIS to map the birth rates of teenage mothers by block groups, and then overlaid that data with information on available resources to support the young mothers. The obvious disparity between needs and resources led to new thinking about resource allocation in the county (Greene 2000).

Policy decisions by external entities significantly impact the use of geospatial technology. For example, the Government Accounting Standards Board (GASB) has established new requirements for identifying assets required for financial reporting (GASB Statement No. 34). As a result, local governments increasingly have chosen to map their public works infrastructure and inventories and tie them to financial packages to meet the GASB requirements. How the data and tools are leveraged to meet these policy changes reflects the planning and procedures put in place for a community GIS.

Local GIS activity can also be impacted by policy decisions at state and federal levels. For instance, to meet the requirements under the National Pollutant Discharge Elimination System (NPDES 1990), GIS, GPS, and remote sensing locates and maps stormwater infrastructure and characterizes the imperviousness of land. The organizational framework and reporting capabilities of GIS make for an effective tool to address this federal stormwater program mandate.

While GIS supports better governance and policy development for a community, the other side of the equation is that developing a GIS requires considerable political motivation. The decision to implement GIS and other spatial technologies actually drives policy changes for local governments. Because GIS represents geography without borders, governments must cooperate within and beyond their own boundaries. Local governments must adopt new policies if the costs and responsibilities of a GIS are to be shared cooperatively with other governments. Such a collaborative model requires the governance of the GIS to be as carefully planned and structured for success as the technological configuration. The system implementation plan must balance the responsibilities and benefits between collaborating entities. In such instances, failure of a GIS is not limited to the programmer or the analyst. Failure causes enormous political friction. By highlighting the advantages of cooperation through improved and seamless service delivery, managers keep the focus on programmatic successes that support better governance and policy development.

Public information and community engagement

The Internet revolutionized not only the way people access information, but it also changed their expectations of what type of information they can get and how quickly they can get it. These changes continue to have a profound impact on the way local government conducts its business.

For example, new large tract land development plans always seem to spark considerable debate. Most land developers submit plans and graphic displays encompassing only their project area. Frequently, citizens and politicians do not have a complete picture of the relative size and proximity of these proposed projects until after the plans have been approved by a planning commission. The impact on neighbors is often realized only after the local planning or permitting agency has incorporated the development plan into the larger context of surrounding communities.

Using GIS to incorporate plans from home builders, utility construction, and business development into the larger community layout, citizens and elected officials have a tool to evaluate the context of proposed projects. Providing this type of information via the Internet makes government processes public to a level previously unseen *(figure 6.6)*. By providing more information earlier in the approval process, local governance accountability increases along with citizen input. Fewer holdups encountered at the end of any bureaucratic approval process promote efficiencies as well as citizen and business relations.

Figure 6.6   GIS technology allows local governments to show the impact of a proposed development in relationship to community surroundings. This allows residents to have a much better sense of how the development will fit into their community.

Source: Richland County, S.C.

Through geographic information and a growing array of GIS applications, government operations are improving and becoming more tightly integrated in public policy and decision making (Greene 2000). As this transition occurs, citizens also become more integrated in the decision-making process through improved communication. Since using online GIS applications requires no formal training, citizens can enjoy easy access to geospatial information related to their health and safety, government services delivery, and ever-changing characteristics of their community. Armed with such robust information, citizens efficiently affect change through collective engagement on a variety of issues (Craig et al. 2002). In becoming a part of everyday life, GIS provides a vital connection between the governing and the governed.

Managing change in GIS technology

A GIS is an important tool for managing change in a community, but as an emerging technology, its development must also be managed. To do this effectively, it is important to first understand the general evolution of GIS within the local government context and how that will likely affect future use of the technology.

Evolution of GIS

When GIS first came to local government, it most often arrived as a result of a specific thematic need in one department or another. Making the case for GIS investment frequently focused on the operational benefits derived for uses such as E-911 (Enhanced 911 that pinpoints the locations of emergency call from mobile phones), property appraisal, and tax assessment (Mitchell 1997; Greene 2000). The tangible benefits in improved service delivery helped sell the new technology. Many funding opportunities also respond to specific community needs. Grants promoting GIS use target issues such as public safety, social services, health care, and education. The specific use approach aided the diffusion of geospatial technologies by bringing geography-based decision making to the fore. Certainly emergency management and public safety have benefited from this approach. Recent media coverage has also highlighted the use of GIS, GPS, and in-field computing for applications in other small and often overlooked departments such as mosquito control (Wilson 2004).

However, GIS touches on almost all government functions, and programmatic successes continue to introduce the technology to an ever wider audience. Based on the successes of a single-use system in one department, other departments will begin to explore possible uses of the technology. Once local government professionals understand how the power of the technology can be leveraged to organize business practices around a common theme, it is like a light bulb going on. When that happens, requests for maps and Web sites are replaced by questions of how to change procedures to attach geography to data. As department directors realize that GIS is more than making a map, demand for the technology increases.

Technology alone does not effect positive change. To effectively use GIS and related technologies, managers must change the practices and procedures within departmental operations. Buying new software and providing training without reviewing and updating the underlying procedures to accommodate new business practices results only in automating old methods. GIS is an instrument of change, not change itself. Resistance to or slowed methodological change impedes system implementation. Only when GIS is assimilated into the process of a department can its implementation be successful (Cullis 1994).

GIS does provide an opportunity to create change. By beginning a dialog about how daily business practices can be revised and updated to take advantage of this new technology, GIS enables organizations to achieve greater efficiencies. As noted earlier, GIS often begins as a single-use system in an individual department within local government. But once these greater efficiencies are achieved, it does not remain there. As more departments request access to the technology, the GIS may be nurtured into an enterprise operation. Enterprise GIS shifts the focus to results that benefit the entire organization and allows "the organization's members to access and integrate GIS data across all departments" (Tomlinson 2003). Recently, however, a growing number of local governments simply invest in GIS with an eye toward the larger governance perspective. Although it is difficult and requires significant cooperation across all departments, several good examples exist of true enterprise-wide implementation. No matter the route taken, enterprise GIS is fast becoming the norm for local governments.

Interestingly, as enterprise GIS becomes more common, the pressure to apply GIS in thematic departments also increases. Thus, what started in individual departments and is growing to change the institution of government tends to refocus attention on areas not yet exploiting the technology. Numerous professional groups report the ongoing proliferation of GIS in their disciplines. Publications from *Public Works Magazine* and *Roads & Bridges* to *Civil Engineering News* and *Pipeline & Gas Journal* have heralded the emergence of GIS in their respective professions (Rodriquez and Wint 2002; Biver and Isley 2002; Kennedy 2002; Wolicki 2002). The pressure is to spread the technology into more and more government operations. In addition, as the technology becomes more business focused, the complexity of system development and maintenance increases.

Planning and implementing an enterprise GIS must consider all departments and functions of a government. Not dismissing the individual benefits to departments and citizens, a major advantage of an enterprise system is the availability of consistent information across the institution (Tomlinson 2003). As more disciplines adopt GIS, local governments should make an effort to harness the power of related data through coordination.

The trend toward enterprise GIS has a significant impact on local government procedures and practices in some fairly sophisticated ways. For example, many database vendors routinely design components specifically for handling spatial data (Farley 2004). Incorporating geography into core business systems for local governments has only just begun. Previously, most integration with core business or thematic applications occurred through linking data elements to GIS data at the end of system development. The current trend is to consider geography in the needs assessment and scoping stages of a system development project. Because it makes more sense to build on or with GIS than to attach to it later, department directors and information technology (IT) personnel are researching spatial technologies and including them in the design process. The additional functionality provided by geography is being leveraged in practical ways such as spatial query and analyses by employees in call centers, planning departments, utilities, and engineering divisions. One of the first questions asked of any citizen calling for service is the location. Where is the stray dog? Where is the pothole? Where did the accident occur? Almost every call coming into local government call centers requires location information or geographic analysis to respond.

The stability and power of an enterprise system relies on the core dataset. A fundamental set of data themes must be constructed to get off the ground. The most common first layers of a community GIS are digital orthorectified aerial photos, the street network, and land parcels. Many additional layers can be derived from this set. Examples include surface hydrography digitized from aerial imagery, political subdivisions and service zones from the street network, and property value and zoning layers from land parcels. Once the data foundation is in place, professionals in other departments begin to develop new thematic layers for their own operations.

The key to leveraging all of these thematic layers in an enterprise is the relationship between databases. The financial and budget systems do not have to be built on the geographic framework but should be able to link to property and assets. To do this, each asset or property (geography) must have a digital key linking it to business and citizens records. Once that connection is established and maintained, enterprise GIS can be employed to direct business functions such as business licensing, permitting, inspections, and utility billing. Attaching geography to business functions often results in hard dollar cost savings and increased revenues. For example, by managing sewer billing on a per-parcel basis through GIS, National City, California, saved $960,000 in the first year of system implementation (Keese 2004). Similar examples will multiply as local governments continue to make the connection between geography and business practices.

Practicality is the key to success in applying GIS to various government operations. When developing GIS applications for thematic disciplines, an important rule to remember is to avoid using technology for the sake of using technology. Just because it can be done does not mean it should. Unfortunately, there are many examples of this trap. If a storm drain is clogged, should the public works department develop an application for citizens to log onto the county GIS Web site and locate the identification number of the clogged drain before calling the county? Of course not. When a storm drain is clogged, citizens pick up the phone and call the county or city. Do biologists really need to update the mosquito breeding database using wireless communications before they return to the office? Probably not. The key is to evaluate the most practical use of geospatial technology in order to realize the greatest return on investment (ROI).

Finally, the concept of return on investment must be included in GIS planning and implementation. Unfortunately, little consideration has been given to this practice, and it is infrequently presented in GIS education and training programs. Gadgetry may sell or hype a technology, but saving time, lives, and money drives its adoption into routine practice and procedures. Thus, GIS education must introduce or expand the philosophy of quantifiable return on investment strategies as well as practical applications

GIS expertise

In an enterprise system, GIS is a service on which other departments depend. The result is that GIS professionals must be familiar with the thematic needs of the various local government departments. As for GIS users, they often work in departments and disciplines with previously established procedures and techniques. The most effective uses of GIS have come when the two groups intersect, meeting each other half way. The GIS professional learns just enough about a discipline— mosquito control, planning, and stormwater management, among others—and the user learns just enough about the concepts of GIS. This understanding leads to thoughtful questions of needs and appropriate applications, and things start to fall into place.

While this intersection can be extraordinarily productive, it also necessitates some cross training and new interdepartmental procedures. In many locations, health and environment agencies routinely record location information for reporting. Recent advances have provided health professionals with GIS tools to track and mitigate disease outbreaks or vectors. Police officers have also been required to assign resources to target areas based on geographic patterns in reported crime. Each of these practices requires additional education and training focused on the professional needs of the users. The idea is that GIS professionals do not have to become police officers and police officers do not need a degree in geography. But it does require that they have a common understanding of how data will be handled and maintained for the GIS. By exploiting the intersection of previously unrelated concepts such as geography (GIS), biology (mosquito control), and information, GIS professionals can continue to be effective enablers while thematic professionals add capability and efficiency to their practices.

Single-use GIS requires an immediate working group to collect, maintain, analyze, and disseminate data. In moving toward an enterprise solution, such a structure is no longer practical. Many local governments have employed this structure, which is still functional for the smallest of governments. However, having a central group of individuals do this work for all departments in larger and more diverse governments is, at best, inefficient. Training and stewardship are key to implementing enterprise GIS. Personnel in a central GIS shop are not familiar with the thematic details of the various departments' disciplines. On the other hand, engineers, biologists, police officers, and others cannot be expected to do their job while running a department GIS. By meeting in the middle, sophisticated GIS can be leveraged to meet specific departmental goals while supporting the larger enterprise.

When meeting and educating employees in individual departments, GIS professionals must attempt to learn how they do business and understand their specific needs. Sharing an understanding of geospatial technologies often leads to applications not considered by the GIS staff. When the engineer, biologist, and police officer grasp the first concepts of GIS, the questions start rolling and cooperative development begins. As mutual understanding blooms, the GIS manager has a duty to provide the tools and training necessary to achieve the objectives of individual departments. In return, users in each department become responsible for the maintenance of data themes that support the enterprise. The responsibilities of a central GIS department or division include providing initial data, training, and procedures to support stewardship. Coordination can also include disseminating all data layers in user-friendly formats.

In the example depicted in figure 6.7, the GIS division is responsible for developing the foundation layers, defining standards, establishing policies and procedures, providing training, and disseminating data. This central hub of activity has great responsibility but is not tasked with maintaining every thematic layer. For instance, the GIS division may develop the initial street centerline or land parcel layer. Then the division can provide the initial datasets to employees in other departments such as the assessor's office or planning department. With tools, data, training, and new procedures, the employees in these departments begin to maintain data as part of the way they conduct business each day. GIS staff often assists with software and quality control as problems arise. But as the thematic experts, employees in each department become the stewards of their segments of the enterprise.

Stewardship can be distributed to provide an equitable division of labor and assure the integrity of the system *(table 6.1)*. Stewards must truly own the quality assurance process for their own data as part of a larger system. The GIS manager is tasked with gaining this buy-in from each steward. The results are often improved data quality and more informed decision making by individuals in all departments. Efficiencies and cost savings are obvious products. For example, enterprise GIS provides road construction and paving stewards with information about all recorded features within a project area. Fire hydrant and survey monument locations impact paving projects. Without data on site locations easily available, below-grade survey monuments in the right-of-way frequently were paved over and rendered useless. When all departments share geographic data, engineers and contractors can avoid such costly mistakes and feature location information can be incorporated into the construction plan.

Data stewards must be able to accomplish their maintenance tasks as a part of their departmental business process. Recording and managing data cannot be additional work. Thus, the processes of everyday tasks must include spatial data recoding. As any change may be unwelcome in the business of other departments, the review of existing practices and recommendation of GIS-enabled procedures must be accepted as having value or providing improvement. This single step moving from task-specific GIS to a spatially-enabled government enterprise is the most difficult aspect of system implementation. Changing business procedures is at the core of most encountered resistance while offering the greatest potential to make government more efficient. GIS, as stated by U.S. Congressman Adam Putnam at the 2004 ESRI Federal User Conference, "challenges our traditional way of organizing government" (Schutzberg 2004).

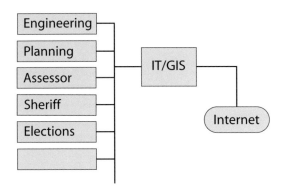

Figure 6.7 GIS implementation in local government varies by jurisdiction. Centralized development with distributed thematic stewardship is depicted here.

Source: Richland County, S.C.

Table 6.1 Clarifying lines of communications and responsibilities for maintaining data within the GIS, such as those represented here, helps circumvent confusion and improves overall efficiency.		
Thematic Department	**Data Stewardship Responsibility**	**Update Frequency**
IT/GIS	Ortho Imagery	As Needed
Assessor	Parcels	Daily
Planning	Street Addresses	Daily
	Landcover	As Needed
	Buildings	Daily
Zoning	Zoning Designation	As Needed
Engineering	Streets	Daily
	Elevation	As Needed
	Hydrography	As Needed
	Geodetic Control	As Needed
Sheriff	Patrol Zones	As Needed
	Crime	Daily
Elections	Voter Precincts	As Needed
	Poling Locations	As Needed

Source: Richland County, S.C.

The breadth of knowledge required to effectively develop and maintain an operational enterprise GIS has outstripped the capacity of single individuals. Training and education have not kept pace with rapidly advancing technologies. Human resources have always been mentioned as a component of GIS; however, they are quickly becoming the one component that most often will slow a system down or minimize effectiveness. As for the future of the GIS professionals in local government, their numbers will only increase. The U.S. Department of Labor has identified geospatial technologies one of three technologies facing explosive growth over the next decade (Sietzen 2004).

But GIS professionals must wear many hats. Beyond a general knowledge base of local government operational systems, they must be the resident experts in GIS and any related spatial technology such as GPS and remote sensing. The burden expands dramatically when the GIS sits on a complex database and in feature data models. Their field of expertise must then expand to database management and computer science. Furthermore, if an Internet mapping application is necessary, the needed skill sets expand to computer networking and Internet development. These requirements are all on top of the earliest misconceptions that GIS personnel are also the office IT technicians. The body of knowledge required has expanded to desktop computers, servers, in-field devices, software, and media. As technology evolves and GIS becomes its own governmental infrastructure, such requirements will continue to expand.

In addition to technical requirements, GIS personnel are also becoming more involved in procurement, contracting, and legal agreements. The GIS staff may be asked to review proposals for cable franchising, cell tower permitting contracts, and intergovernmental agreements. How can these high expectations be managed? There is no single answer. Solutions include cross-training with other departments, hiring additional staff or consultants, and outsourcing. Management must be able to support these individuals or departments when limited expertise in any of these areas is identified. The important point is that management recognizes the expectations placed on GIS personnel and the significant and diverse body of knowledge required to effectively develop and maintain an enterprise system.

Legal issues

As with any technological development, legal issues always crop up as new applications become available. The majority of legal battles regarding GIS are fought over data issues. Local governments seem to be on the front lines of this topic. Unfortunately, most GIS professionals, managers, and local government attorneys are not prepared to engage in the discussion. Making matters worse, GIS capabilities are being evaluated using laws that do not directly address geospatial digital data and electronic communications issues.

With the ability to intersect previously disparate information, GIS has prompted numerous concerns regarding personal privacy. Making public records easily accessible via the Internet concerns citizens who prefer items such as marriage licenses and property records remain as paper documents in a courthouse. Attaching geography to accessible public records increases the public's concerns. Local government has chosen diverse methods to address privacy issues. Some local governments allow Internet property searches using owner name and provide information such as assessed value, amount of taxes paid and when, sale price, and even floor plans and photographs.[1] Other local governments limit name searches and do not include information beyond tabular items describing assessed value, zoning, and sales data. The decision of how much data is made available online and tied to geography falls to the discretion of individual cities and counties. In making this decision, managers must balance the capabilities of technology with the wishes of citizens and the elected body.

The legal arguments encompassing the privacy issue are often related to the concept of open government records or public information. The balance between public records availability and privacy remains a moving target in most locations. One argument is that all public records should be made available through the Internet, while another perspective seeks to make documents available, but only at the courthouse. The issue comes down to access. Does making existing public records more accessible infringe on the privacy of individual citizens? Local governments across the country are struggling with this question. Few laws have been passed to specifically address privacy related to public records of geography, such as personal property, property taxation, and deeds, to name a few.

The concept of public records has also impacted the dissemination of GIS data collected by local governments. Many states have not specifically addressed geospatial data in their open records laws. However, recognizing privacy concerns and potential value of geospatial information, several states have updated their open records laws to accommodate either broader distribution of or limited access to GIS data. Some argue that regardless of the type of information, all government data must be made available on request. Opposing opinions point out the commercial value of data collected and caution against supporting private industry via tax-sponsored programs.

Most states allow local governments to recoup the cost of reproduction for requested data. Even this simple notion can be clouded when GIS data holdings are maintained in sophisticated data models and encompass terabytes of storage. In 2001, the state of Georgia amended its open records law to permit governments to distribute GIS data on a fee basis that includes recovery of system development (GA 2001). A more centrist path was taken by the state of Maryland in that GIS data ". . .developed at public expense should not be unreasonably withheld from private commercial users of geographic information, but should not provide a public subsidy to private commercial users" (Code of Maryland Regulations, 10-902). A variety of philosophies that intersect with privacy and data management are guiding these policies.

In summary, restricting the distribution of or licensing GIS data is becoming a significant topic in privacy, freedom of information, and funding discussions. Local government managers must recognize the depth of the discussion, and formulate a corporate strategy and associated policy that fits the governance and social structure of their community.

Related to availability and dissemination of data is the issue of GIS data use liability. Local governments have been proactive on liability by creating appropriate metadata and accompanying liability statements. Most GIS Web sites and map products include statements declaring limitations on data use and liability. Although proper metadata can address this item with information regarding appropriate use, formal statements must accompany all data products whether hard copy or digital.

Other emerging legal issues include data access limitations due to homeland security efforts and licensure to practice. Although data access issues related to homeland security are most often driven by policy beyond local government, they do impact how GIS data is maintained and disseminated. Local GIS managers most likely will be made aware of the implications to operations as they arise. As for who can and cannot use GIS, technology access has been defined by individuals outside of GIS who successfully restrict use of the technology via professional licensure. In a few states, specific uses of GIS and GPS have been limited by requiring licensure as a professional surveyor (SC 2000). Complaints have been filed against local government GIS personnel for using GPS to locate fire hydrants (Pendleton 2002). Local government GIS professionals in states that require licensure must research and understand limitations on their activities. Legal issues are often addressed *a priori* in response to immediate concerns, such as liability or licensure. Thus, along with a long list of other nontechnical duties, GIS professionals must remain aware of tangential legal issues that may impact their operations, and then rely on staff attorneys or seek outside assistance when necessary.

Standards

Discussions involving standards in any industry will cite established rules by national or international groups that pertain to everyday work. This is also true of GIS. However, unlike many professions, what is most important for the user are local or corporate standards. Local standards, or those on which individual business practices are based, must be developed to produce expected and repeatable results. This is most important as few local governments employ identical procedures. From standardized or uniform output, information may

Freedom of information (FOI) laws and data security

State freedom of information (FOI) laws generally recognize the importance of access to computerized public records and guarantee the public's right to request electronic FOI disclosure. But does that give the public the right to access all GIS data and images maintained by a jurisdiction? In the past few years, several states have amended their individual FOI laws to exempt GIS data from disclosure or allow government agencies to recoup GIS-related costs. The arguments and decisions related to the difference between data and information will continue as technology and its application outpace appropriate funding mechanisms and legal precedent.

Local governments across the country are struggling to address this issue and are engaged in court cases to sort out the intended extent of the FOI laws. At issue is whether local governments can legally restrict the public's access to electronic GIS data as a matter of community, system, or financial security. The author approached several local governments to prepare a case study on this issue and were turned down repeatedly due to its hotly contested nature. Since this issue must be resolved on a state-by-state basis, the privacy, security, and funding debate over making GIS data widely available will likely continue for some time.

Prepared by Patrick Bresnahan, geographic information officer for Richland County, S.C.

be mapped to a higher standard or converted automatically by vendors implementing national or international standards.

Standards related to GIS may be divided into several categories. There are standards for hardware components, software, measurements, databases, data models, data exchange, and procedures. Other standards related to hardware, software, databases, and data exchange are established by national or international organizations or the private sector, and often do not impact individual users. In short, there is no one group or organization responsible for setting standards in the field. Rather, a number of groups work on a variety of standards related to the technology.

For example, groups such as the World Wide Web Consortium (W3C) and the International Organization for Standardization (ISO) develop technologies and standards for many issues. Only a fraction of their work concerns GIS. Interoperable technologies developed and approved by W3C are used to run intranet, Internet, and wireless applications for every technology. However, applications of geospatial data are accommodated in projects such as scalable vector graphics (SVG). This programming concept has potential for sharing vector GIS data efficiently via the Internet. ISO works on several dozen sets of standards on topics ranging from feature identification using coordinates to location-based services (ISOTC 211 2004). Results from working groups defining ISO standards are often adopted by national groups such as American National Standards Institute (ANSI), software and hardware vendors, and data developers. The Open GIS Consortium, Inc. (OGC) has focused on creating open spatial programming and application structures to provide increased access to GIS data and analyses by removing translation barriers and proprietary elements. Such standards are often not apparent to local government professionals as they are incorporated in data and software products prior to procurement. However, knowledge of these standards is useful when procuring and contracting to assure compatibility with existing components.

More relevant to local government GIS are the set of national standards being developed by the Federal Geographic Data Committee (FGDC). As a committee staffed primarily by federal stakeholders, the majority of standards developed by FGDC are applicable primarily to countrywide datasets and procedures. However, some FGDC activities translate well to all levels of GIS application. FGDC standards particularly relevant at the local level apply to metadata, thematic data layer content, data classification, data transfer, and positional accuracy. Although metadata is often overlooked, the standard allows information about GIS to be shared seamlessly ensuring appropriate use and minimizing data overlay errors. Local governments also have much to gain by reviewing content standards for fundamental thematic layers such as hydrography, parcels, and imagery. The breadth of the content standards is overwhelming for most GIS professionals, but pertinent elements may be extracted to support local government data.

More important than federal standards, local standards are the foundation on which the enterprise GIS depends. Before analyses and dissemination can be executed, data layers must align with each other in a common coordinate framework. This concept is paramount given that geography does not stop at the county line. Thus, GIS data should be continuous and contiguous across all administrative boundaries. Spatial reference standards should be defined early in development. The unit of measure, projection, datum, and conversion methods should all be standardized throughout the organization. Standardized data representation and attribution is just as important. When two adjoining governments maintain GIS-based street address files using the same standards, data becomes seamless across political boundaries. Not adhering to standards limits the potential of GIS application among many users. It is best if all standards are clearly defined prior to system development and included in the GIS implementation plan. However, as user needs and measurement technologies improve, some of the parameters may require adjustment. For example, the horizontal datum used in many states has been continuously updated with the help of GPS and reference station technologies. A judgment must be made as to when or if the enterprise data will be adjusted for these incremental improvements.

As local government enterprise GIS expands, significant attention should be paid to standardizing procedures. The development and implementation of procedural standards supports quality data collection and use. They must address business practices within thematic departments as well as across the enterprise. Data entry and update must be coordinated as to assure quality and limited error propagation. Without standard data collection procedures, defining the accuracy of datasets becomes extremely difficult.

Procedural standards also affect citizens and private enterprise doing business with the local government authority (McGray 2001). This observation is confirmed by the growing number of local government permitting entities that require documents to be submitted in standard formats. Requiring digital submission of land development plans fosters immediate efficiencies in document flow and plan review. Data from disparate sources are delivered to the permitting agency and can be reviewed without concern for differences in feature identification and scale. With standardized layers and geographic coordinates, not only can a development

Figure 6.8   Local government GIS requires a standardized approach to data collection and editing to ensure features are maintained efficiently and effectively. For example, street names and address ranges for roads that exist, are under construction, or are proposed help with the review of development plans.

Source: Richland County, S.C.

plan be reviewed more quickly, it can also be reviewed in the context of the surrounding geography. In addition to increasing operational efficiency, this process speeds the delivery of information to county staff, businesses, and citizens. Proposed features and those under construction, such as roads, can be displayed through GIS as exhibited in figure 6.8. This single procedural standard also represents a step forward in geospatial data and analyses, becoming a part of the business practices of various professions.

Local governments must be proactive in standard development. Development of high-level standards may be left to academic and commercial groups as they will be applied universally. However, local standards help change local practices. Only when local standards are applied can business methods be changed to include digital data.

Technologies

Technological innovation and improvement seem to be the most visible components of GIS that require change management. As data collection and recording technologies improve, the amount of information that must be stored and analyzed grows exponentially. Increased volumes of data require planning and management to assure effective use of new and updated information. The time required to display a 30-meter image on a desktop computer may seem excessive until the thirty-meter image is replaced with one-foot resolution imagery of the same area. How long is too long to have users wait for data to display on a screen? Hardware and software upgrades are pushed by the need to efficiently use the ever-expanding volumes of GIS data.

Other upgrades are prompted by vendors. The upgrade cycle of contemporary software keeps professionals on their toes. In a change from the early days of GIS, software is frequently licensed and distributed before the products are completely stable. Bug fixes and patches become a way of life for GIS practitioners. The pitch for increased functionality in the next version helps to drive this cycle. If managing a changing technological environment is a problem, it seems to be a good problem to have. Once users comprehend the value of local government GIS, they tend to want more. Users become GIS "addicts" who crave more data and want it updated more frequently than economically feasible. This trend seems to catch many local government managers off guard. Once a GIS presence has been established, the demand for increases in data collection and dissemination become a significant burden. This may be a good problem to have, but managers must be prepared to deal with it.

The pace of technological change is moving faster than many governments can manage. As locals adopt new data types, software, and hardware, they realize the next best thing is out and being pushed by vendors. Many advances are incremental and can be bothersome to keep up with while others can be exploited to vastly improve operations. In addition, most local GIS professionals are quite busy with implementation or serving users and have little time to research new technologies. Technological change puts tremendous pressure on human resources, which is driving increased outsourcing for specialized projects and activities. GIS management must concentrate on implementation and operations, but should remain engaged in user groups and professional societies to evaluate new technology as it is presented.

Trends in technological development that most impact local government GIS include improvements in data collection and conversion, data management, and user applications. Over the past decade, local governments have taken advantage of new technologies, such as scanners, digital imaging, and GPS, that are becoming commonplace. Data conversion has moved from digitizing tablets to scanners while data collection has benefited from improved GPS capabilities that link locations to databases. Although evolving technology has made data collection more efficient, it has also increased the amount of information collected. This result improves decision making through higher resolution and more frequently updated data. However, it has also required enhanced data management and dissemination methods.

Data collection technologies are expanding recorded spatial information to previously unimaginable volumes. Digital land cameras already can record GPS information with each image. Video and audio data linked to location is continuously collected, requiring enormous storage capacities. Limiting such recording to pertinent features using visual and audio cues will begin to pare the amount of data collected as such technology is improved. Autonomous data loggers and gauges populate GIS databases without human intervention. These devices have also expanded the volume of recorded spatial data. This trend will continue as advanced measurement devices are developed.

Even more overwhelming than increased volumes of spatial information from *in situ* measurement is the amount of data collected from remote sensing platforms. Current commercial satellite products can be purchased on demand and include multiple bands of image data at resolutions as fine as 62 centimeters. Recently developed aircraft imaging systems deliver digital aerial images (not photographs) at resolutions approaching 2 to 3 inches. These systems deliver data in multiple spectral bands that benefit automated feature analyses and extraction. Local governments acquiring such data must consider the data management requirements of delivered products. A 16-bit, 5,000-by-5,000-foot file of imagery (source is 12-bit) that includes the red, green, blue, and near-infrared portions of the spectrum at 1-foot ground resolution exceeds 200 megabytes! These characteristics will only increase as hyperspectral and lidar technologies reach saturation in the data collection market. Local governments must diligently specify product requirements and plan well ahead of delivery for the storage, management, and use of such large datasets, which can limit productivity if not handled efficiently. The future of data collection will only bring more spatial data at higher resolutions more frequently.

With the size of data holdings increasing exponentially, data models and management must also keep pace. As government staff and citizens request more from their enterprise GIS, managers will be required to expand capabilities. Computer components, including storage, networks, processing, and display will increase in speed to accommodate the growing volume of data. Database technologies and business systems have discovered geospatial data as a rich vein to be mined. To take advantage of GIS, database technologies are evolving to incorporate geographic data in corporate environments while limiting the complexity of applications. Most business system users will not need to know much about geography to use spatial data in such systems. To advance this concept, data models will improve to incorporate fuzzy boundaries as well as three- and four-dimensional features. Using a system that depicts geography in a more life-like context decreases the need for special end-user training.

With more data delivered at faster rates, new applications will be required by GIS users. Local government enterprises will expand their offerings to internal users as well as to the public. Wireless technology has brought GIS to phones and cars. The key to local government participation in this trend is quality geospatial data. Without accurate and up-to-date data, handheld GIS or other delivery devices are of limited use. Private firms do not collect street and property data as part of their business practices. Local governments will be pressured to make their GIS open enough to be leveraged by a variety of value-added applications. Local data will be instantaneously incorporated into public applications for navigation, situational awareness, advertising, public safety, and other profitable enterprises. It is at that intersection of local government implementation and consumer use that GIS will be a part of everyday life.

The road ahead

The successful application of geospatial technologies in an expanding number of government departments will result in a broadened adoption of common practices with unique objectives. As departments adopt GIS and become both data users and data stewards, daily tasks and procedures will evolve to leverage spatial analyses in service delivery and governance. It is only when GIS is assimilated into these functions, and not thrown

Going mobile in Worthington, Minnesota

Winters in Minnesota generally mean lots of snow and ice. For the City of Worthington, snow and ice once meant municipal utility workers having difficulty finding water main valves in an emergency. That problem, along with a desire to improve its entire maintenance program, led the Worthington Public Utilities to invest in a mobile GIS/GPS system.

Plans call for the utility workers to survey the entire water infrastructure for the city. Rather than record the locations of fire hydrants, water valves, and other system components on paper for later entry in a computer database, the GPS technology removes the written transcription process entirely. Using a handheld computer, work crews pinpoint their location on a map and record it directly into a geocoded database. For example, while standing next to the fire hydrant, employees can enter location coordinates, take a digital photo, note mechanical and physical condition of the component, manufacturer, model, year built, and depth of bury, among other variables. With this data collected and then stored in a GIS, future projects can be planned in the office, eliminating many of the survey activities that have been repeated over the years.

Likewise, the utility also plans to survey the entire electric system in Worthington. With that data, the utility can work on connectivity within the system quickly and accurately, displaying primary lines and determining which customers are connected to which line. In a power outage, this information becomes vital in locating customers without service. In short, the new system means better planning, better maintenance, and ultimately better service for the residents of Worthington.

Based on an interview with and materials provided by Eric Roos, water superintendent, Worthington Public Utilities.

The next dimension: GIS goes 3D in Milford Township, Pennsylvania

Planners and community developers have used GIS to better envision the impact of land-use changes for more than three decades. GIS has been especially useful in managing growth and controlling urban sprawl by creating alternative build-out scenarios for communities. But until very recently, growth has primarily been considered in the horizontal, not the vertical, sense. Things like building height, floor-to-area ratios, and sunlight requirements have received little consideration in developing land-use plans. New GIS technology, which creates a three-dimensional image of buildings and spaces, is changing all that.

According to a team of researchers at the Center for Sustainable Communities at Temple University in Pennsylvania, 3D GIS helps identify natural and historic resources that give a community its unique sense of place. By identifying areas in and around a community that should be preserved for their historic and environmental value, community residents can see the potential results of alternative development scenarios.

The researchers selected Milford Township in southeastern Pennsylvania as a test case for using 3D GIS to prepare alternative build-out scenarios for the community. The team first determined Milford's build-out capacity by taking into account
- Land-use designations—agricultural preservation, airport buffer zones, wetlands, and similar protected areas
- Density specifications—number of dwelling units per acre, lot size, floor space, etc.
- Land-use efficiency—an assigned value that considers how much land is lost to development
- Building-placement constraints—soil types, infrastructure requirements, zoning district, etc.

Ultimately, the team came up with three-dimensional simulations of two development alternatives. The first scenario looked at areas in the township zoned for high density use and considered optimal for dense development. Under this scenario, the researchers found that 2,171 new buildings could be incorporated into the township without losing any of the essential elements of the local landscape. The second scenario spread development more evenly throughout the township and converted one acre of rural development zoning into a higher density use. This scenario produced 1,896 new buildings for the township.

The next dimension: GIS goes 3D in Milford Township, Pennsylvania (cont.)

The end results of these two scenarios clearly show that the township is affected by a number of environmental and physical constraints, assuming its citizens want to preserve the general landscape of the community and their unique sense of place. The three-dimensional GIS representations of the two development alternatives offer a concrete sense of how today's choices will affect tomorrow's environment.

Based on "Growth management plan for Milford Township, PA: Suitability analysis and build-out scenarios" by Mahbubur Rabb Meenar, Abdul Bari, and Jesse Sherry, a paper presented at the 2004 ESRI International User Conference, August 9–13, 2004 in San Diego, Calif.

a   b

Figures 6.9a and b The Center for Sustainable Communities at Temple University developed two potential development scenarios for Milford Township in Pennsylvania using a 3D GIS application. The alternative scenarios give residents a sense of how their community could grow depending on land use and density choices they adopt.

Source: Center for Sustainable Communities, Temple University, Penn.

on top of existing procedures, that the technology becomes empowering. Regardless of discipline or service department, the most effective local GIS will continue to be one that becomes part of the governing process and remains transparent to the user.

As geospatial technologies evolve in public and private-sector applications, the business of local government is changing to exploit the overwhelming benefits of integration and analysis of geographic information. Such change is accompanied by increased expectations from citizens and other government entities. Citizens and local businesses have come to rely on spatially-referenced data available on the Internet for personal and professional needs. These users have already changed the way they do business and continue to ask for additional data and increased functionality.

Beyond community-based applications, state and federal agencies recognize that local government is the source of the most up-to-date and highest resolution spatial data. Thus, state and federal government geospatial efforts are beginning to focus on local government GIS to exploit existing foundations on which national and global systems can be built. Developing a national spatial data infrastructure most certainly depends on the success of local government systems (Williamson et al. 2003).

With respect to data development, standards, procedures, and practical applications, local governments are far ahead of state and federal cooperative efforts and will play a major role in the evolution of the technology

(Hissong 1999). Local GIS efforts have also experienced the most change and, in many cases, have managed this dynamic technology successfully. The trend of successful change management throughout system implementation has led to an unanticipated elevation of prominence among geospatial professionals within government administration (Romeo 2004).

With more local governments adopting GIS and its impact on political and social agendas, addressing new legal issues will become a higher priority. Furthermore, as new technologies are developed, managers must continue to evaluate their appropriate application to gain the greatest return on GIS investment for all. Thus, as the complexity of the technology and its application increases, so will the expectations placed upon local government GIS managers.

With an ever-expanding role in governance and service delivery, it is inevitable that GIS will become part of everyday life. Reflecting on the breadth of GIS application in daily governing practices, it won't be long before GIS melts into the ordinary and becomes a part of everyday life.

Profile—Community profile	
Location	Hawaii
Size (miles square)	600 square miles
Population	902,704 (2003)
Form of government	Mayor-council
Annual GIS operating budget	$650,000
Employees in GIS unit	12.0 FTEs
Governmental departments using GIS	16

Overview

Honolulu, Hawaii, has one of the most advanced local government GIS in the country. The combined city and county government has sought to maximize the efficiency of its service delivery through technology, and its GIS has had a significant role in providing new and expanded services to residents.

Background

Local government leaders in Honolulu first explored the development of a GIS in 1983 and started the system five years later. The decision to implement GIS stemmed from the need to have better property information for land-use regulation and planning efforts. Top administrators in utility management and public safety also had significant interest in the system.

Administrators and managers from throughout the local government formed a GIS executive committee and developed an implementation strategy for the new program. When a GIS coordinator came on board in 1990, the program moved from very basic data deliveries to full-fledged GIS applications that allowed people to retrieve tax assessment and property ownership information.

From that beginning, the system has continued to expand. Ken Schmidt, GIS coordinator with Honolulu's Land Information System, which manages the enterprise, said GIS has developed in incremental stages in Honolulu. Some stages have occurred very rapidly and others somewhat slower. Advances in GIS technology tend to be a driver, leading to new applications and data layers.

Technology at work: Three GIS applications

Among Honolulu's GIS applications is a building footprint geodatabase project. Landscape and physical environment are critical in an island setting, especially with tourism as the primary industry. The geodatabase enables a user to experience 3D spatial information for buildings, including fly-through animations. The initial neighborhoods and areas slated for inclusion in the geodatabase include downtown, Kakaako, Waikiki, and Diamond Head.

The geodatabase allows details of building shapes, roof morphology, and realistic texturing from aerial photography to be captured and visualized using the GIS. This information enables decision makers and local planners to preserve a sense of place and establish an appropriate neighborhood atmosphere when considering building proposals. The new GIS application gives a much greater sense than typical two-dimensional maps of how proposed developments will fit into an area. And it enables policy makers to tailor land-use regulations to permit the best use of properties, allowing for better overall spatial policy.

In-depth case study
Honolulu, Hawaii

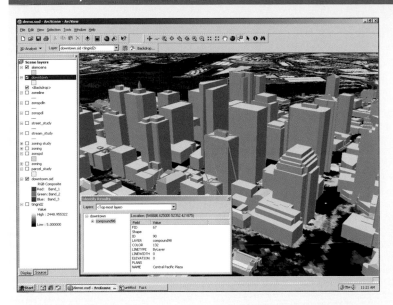

Figure 6.10 The city and county of Honolulu use 3D GIS technology to develop better land-use policy based on a spatial analysis of buildings.

Source: City and county of Honolulu, Hawaii, Honolulu Land Information System

The 3D applications also greatly benefit the island's public safety and police planning programs. The Honolulu Police Department (HPD) uses the systems' analytic capabilities to better visualize the potential impact of catastrophic events such as earthquakes, gas main breaks, and terrorist attacks, and to prepare for natural disasters, including tsunamis and hurricanes. The HPD also uses the system for line-of-sight analysis when it needs to place officers at major events like parades through Waikiki. Being able to determine appropriate locations in and around buildings will improve the overall security of such events.

a **b**
Figures 6.11a and b Aerial photography, together with the new 3D GIS technology, are used by public safety officials in Honolulu to plan for community events and determine appropriate stationing of police officers to maximize security.

Source: Honolulu Land Information System, Honolulu, Hawaii

Storm drain management is another innovative GIS application in Honolulu. Debris frequently collects in the city and county storm drains, clogging the entire system. When heavy rains come to the island, the drains overflow, flooding streets. The public works department sought a better method for tracking which storm drains were being cleaned and how often. Through this GIS application, department managers can better track which drains tend to become clogged and will ultimately use this information to schedule preventative cleanings.

The application uses bar codes to identify a drain's geographic location. Workers affix a bar-code label on or near each storm drain, either on the manhole cover or somewhere inside near the culvert. When workers go out to the field, they take a handheld computer unit and scan the bar-code label to bring up the geographic identifier for that particular storm drain. After cleaning the drain, crew members record the level of the debris they found and when they cleaned it. Back at the office, they put the unit in a docking station which transfers the data into a database linked to the GIS.

Department managers then use the GIS to look at what type of cleaning has occurred in which locations. An intranet application allows managers to query the data and review where problems routinely occur. The system is also linked into a simplified work management system, which allows the department to better track the results of their work orders and respond to citizens' requests for service.

Businesses have also taken advantage of the data available through the local government GIS. A number of companies produce travel kit computer programs for use on a PDA. A visitor to Honolulu can purchase such a kit, which includes information about city streets and sites of interests. The tourist can identify the hotel where he or she is staying and then get instructions on how to reach a popular tourist destination like Diamond Head. The program produces driving instructions on how to get there from the hotel.

These three GIS applications represent just a few of the ways the technology has changed operations within the local government and the community.

Changes in local government

Technology has definitely changed the way local government does business in Honolulu. GIS is just one component of Honolulu's information technology (IT) effort that has helped drive the changes.

Overall, the GIS allows Honolulu to offer many public services without requiring a staff person to provide them. Residents no longer need to visit government offices to get answers to their questions. They can go online and use a GIS application to find out whether their house is located in a particular flood zone, how their neighborhood is zoned, or details about a piece of property they are interested in purchasing. Just a few years ago, answers to such questions required a resident to schedule an appointment in the office and make a request in person.

Most of the changes have occurred incrementally as technology has evolved. Schmidt explained, "When we first implemented that first GIS user interface, staff could bring the information up, and answer land-use and property questions right over the phone." A phone conversation would last fifteen minutes instead of the thirty to sixty minutes required in a face-to-face meeting. "And now we've got it to where it's on the Internet. People are pulling it up, and they can get those questions answered themselves. They're not even calling," Schmidt said.

Likewise, the GIS has proved its worth to the local business community. Henry Eng, director of Honolulu's planning and permitting department, said, "Local government GIS is good for the business community because it provides critical data to meet a wide range of business needs. The Honolulu GIS is comprehensive yet user-friendly, and it saved me countless hours in my former consultant practice."

Beyond the new services that technology has brought to residents and businesses of Honolulu, it has also changed daily operations within the local government. Together, GIS and IT technology have decentralized the information flow within local government. The information flow is now lateral as well as vertical. Employees no longer need to go to another department to get information a citizen needs; they have easy access to it through the GIS. That accessibility to information has empowered the front-counter employees to respond to citizens directly. Schmidt said, "It has provided an important knowledge base for our local government. By putting information into the hands of the employees who use it, they can better respond and provide better service to the public."

Having easy access to information also saves time for employees. For example, the parks and recreation department's offices are located outside of downtown Honolulu. Before GIS, when employees needed information on facilities located in each of the parks, they had to drive downtown to pick up maps with that information. With Web-based GIS technology, they can get the information off the Internet, including photos.

Staying abreast of new technology

Honolulu has benefited tremendously from GIS, and local government leaders have worked hard to improve the technology's efficiency. But Honolulu is somewhat remote, and staying current on what is happening in the field has its challenges. GIS staff members rely heavily on the Internet and other electronic communications to keep up on the latest trends.

Schmidt stays abreast by attending conferences and seminars, including the ESRI annual user conferences, the URISA (Urban and Regional Information Systems), GIAT (Geospatial Information and Technology Association), and ASPRS (American Society of Photogrammetry and Remote Sensing) conferences. He believes that feedback from other agencies in critical in the development of a local government GIS program. Small conferences and regional meetings are among the best ways to stay in touch with new advances in technology and strengthen a local government GIS program, he said.

Return on investment

Implementing a GIS involves a considerable upfront investment in staff time and money before any benefits are gained. These costs raise serious concerns for local government policy makers who wonder about the return on investment (ROI). Honolulu has conducted a number of costs-benefit assessments to quantify and track its overall ROI in its GIS. The local government's most significant benefits involve better management of data entry, elimination of data redundancies, and improved processes for data retrieval and researching functionalities that support basic city operations. Honolulu estimates it has reduced processing time on these functions by around 20 percent using new technology and methods of doing business.

Honolulu does not, however, make a practice of doing a full cost-benefit analysis before the introduction of every new program. When preparing a justification for a new program or application, the GIS team reviews benefits gained from previous advances and notes expected changes with the release of a new program. Schmidt said that while cost-benefit assessment can be helpful in justifying investments, it is more important "to educate decision makers on where the inefficiencies exist and how technology can eliminate those inefficiencies."

The automation of Honolulu's subdivision mapping program, he said, is an example how GIS technology eliminated some of those inefficiencies. For a number of years, the local government had operated two separate base mapping programs. One program mapped land divisions based on legal subdivisions or regulatory subdivisions for individuals subdividing their properties for development purposes. Another program was used by the tax assessor's office for subdividing or combining parcels for tax assessment purposes. The uses and maps produced by the programs were completely separate, but the data representing the land was

essentially the same, just from two different views. By implementing a new program that combined both functions, the costs for data maintenance were essentially cut in half.

The time frame for expecting a return on investment is largely a matter of how the initial investment is handled. If the initial investment is substantial, returns could start coming within two to three years. But if the initial investment is done incrementally, then the returns will also come incrementally. Schmidt cautioned that measuring the full value of costs and benefits can be challenging. Public services that no longer have to be performed as a result of new technology are very difficult to quantify. On the other hand, he noted that Honolulu's map production program has dropped from eighteen full-time positions to fewer than eight and achieved a cost savings of more than $400,000 per year.

Advice to other local governments

The ultimate success of a local government GIS program is dependent on people at three levels. First, executive champions are needed. These individuals are committed to the GIS and willing to support that commitment with resources. And they will take on the budget battles required to secure resources. Without that commitment, it is difficult to secure the necessary resources.

At the next level are the front-line supervisors of the GIS end users. If these individuals are sold on the benefits of the GIS, they can promote staff acceptance. Having them participate in the development of GIS applications, and assist in outlining requirements of the system, helps secure their buy-in and ensure the long-term success of the program.

The last group is the end users. These individuals are most directly impacted by the GIS. Forming a GIS users group creates a network of proponents for GIS technology. They will serve as advocates for the technology. Perhaps more than any other group, they can speak to the direct benefits of the GIS and how it helps improve their efficiency.

References

Biver, John, and David Isley. 2002. Public feedback, computer input. *Roads & Bridges* 40 (8): 42–43.

Code of Maryland Regulations: 10–901; 10–902. Available online at www.rcfp.org/elecaccess/maryland.htm

Craig, William J., Trevor M. Harris, and Daniel Weiner. 2002. *Community participation and geographic information systems.* London, UK: Taylor & Francis.

Cullis, Brian J. 1994. A Strategy for Assessing Organizational GIS Adoption Success. *GIS/Lis 94 Conference Proceedings,* 208–17.

Farley, Jim. 2004. Oracle 10g: A location-enabled platform for enterprise GIS and core business applications. *Earth Observation Magazine* 13 (3): 29–32.

Georgia, 2001. *Official Code of Georgia*, Chapter 29, Title 50, Section 1.

Government Accounting Standards Board (GASB) Statement No. 34.

Greene, R. W. 2000. *GIS in public policy. Redlands,* Calif.: ESRI Press.

Hissong, Frank. 1999. Will locals lead the way to a national GIS? *American City & County* 114 (9).

ISOTC (International Organization for Standardization Technical Committee) 211. Available online at www.ISO.org

Keese, Karen. 2004. Avoiding sewer rate hikes. *American City & County* 119 (8): 51.

Kennedy, Sheila. 2002. Pipelines benefit by integrating management systems. *Pipeline & Gas Journal* 229 (9): 55–56.

Masser, Ian. 1998. *Governments and geographic information.* London, UK: Taylor & Francis.

McGray, Jerry. 2001. Geodetic surveying made plain: Now everybody's doing it. *Point of Beginning* (POB) 26 (4): 62–64.

Mitchell, Andy. 1997. *Zeroing in: Geographic information systems at work in the community.* Redlands, Calif.: ESRI Press.

NPDES (National Pollutant Discharge Elimination System). 1990. *Code of Federal Regulations* (CFR) Title 40 Part 122 Section 122.23(b)(1).

Pendleton, Greg. 2002. Walking the blurred line of geodesy. *GeoWorld* 15 (6): 28–29.

PTI (Public Technology Institute). 2003. National GIS survey results: 2003 survey on the use of GIS technology in local governments. Washington, D.C.: Public Technology Institute.

Rodriquez, Rene, and Ian Wint. 2002. City switches from a traditional to an object-oriented GIS data model. *Public Works* 133 (10): 90–94.

Romeo, James. 2004. View at the top. *American City & County* 119 (11): 37–41. Available online at americancityandcounty.com/mag/government_view_top.

Salem, Larry et al. 1977. User needs assessment for an operational geographic information system. Washington, D.C.: U.S. Fish and Wildlife Service, U.S. Dept. of the Interior.

Schutzberg, Adena. 2004. Federal GIS users unite at ESRI conference. *Earth Observation Magazine* 13 (2): 16–20.

Sietzen, Frank, Jr. 2004. High-growth jobs initiative. *GeoSpatial Solutions* 14 (6): 20–22.

South Carolina. 2004. *Code of regulations.* Chapter 117–1740.2

South Carolina. 2000. *Code of Laws.* Title 40, Chapter 22, Section 20.

Star, Jeffrey, and John Estes.1990. *Geographic information systems.* Englewood Cliffs, N.J.: Prentice-Hall.

Tomlinson, Roger. 2003. *Thinking about GIS: Geographic information system planning for managers.* Redlands, Calif.: ESRI Press.

Williamson, Ian, Abbas Rajabifard, and Mary-Ellen F. Feeney. 2003. *Developing spatial data infrastructures: From concept to reality.* London, UK: Taylor & Francis.

Wilson, Joey. 2004. West Nile virus: Battlers buzzing about GIS technology. *GeoWorld* 17 (6): 34–36.

Wolicki, Carol. 2002. Geospatial interoperability: How it affects the GIS world and you. *CE News* (July): 36–39.

Resources

A wealth of information exists to help develop a local government GIS program. This resource list highlights just a few sources for learning more about the potential uses for a local government GIS.

Associations and organizations

National associations and organizations provide networking, peer-to-peer assistance, educational opportunities, and other resources to support a local government GIS program.

American Congress on Surveying and Mapping
www.acsm.net
6 Montgomery Village Avenue, Suite 403
Gaithersburg, MD 20879
Phone: (240) 632-9716

American Planning Association
www.planning.org
122 South Michigan Avenue, Suite 1600
Chicago, IL 60603
Phone: (312) 431-9100

American Society for Photogrammetry and Remote Sensing
www.asprs.org
5410 Grosvenor Lane, Suite 210
Bethesda, MD 20814-2160
Phone: (301) 493-0290

Association of American Geographers
www.aag.org
1710 16th Street NW
Washington, DC 20009-3198
Phone: (202) 234-1450

Council of State Governments
www.csg.org
2760 Research Park Drive
P. O. Box 11910
Lexington, KY 40578-1910
Phone: (859) 244-8000

Geospatial Information & Technology Association
www.gita.org
14456 E. Evans Avenue
Aurora, CO 80014
Phone: (303) 337-0513

Government Management Information Sciences
www.gmis.org
P. O. Box 365
Bayville, NJ 08721
Phone: (800) 460-7454 or (973) 632-0470

International Association of Assessing Officers
www.iaao.org
314 W. 10th Street
Kansas City, MO 64105
Phone: (816) 701-8100

International City/County Management Association
www.icma.org
777 North Capitol Street, NE–Suite 500
Washington, D.C. 20002
Phone: (202) 289-4262

Public Technology Institute
www.pti.org
1301 Pennsylvania Avenue, NW–Suite 800
Washington, D.C. 20002
Phone: (202) 289-4262

National Association of Counties
www.naco.org
440 First Street, NW
Washington, D.C. 20001
Phone: (202) 393-6226

National Association of Regional Councils
www.narc.org
1666 Connecticut Avenue, NW–Suite 300
Washington, D.C. 20009
Phone: (202) 986-1032

National Conference of State Legislatures
www.ncsl.org
444 North Capitol Street, NW–Suite 515
Washington, D.C. 20001
Phone: (202) 624-5400

National Governors' Association
www.nga.org
Hall of States
444 N. Capitol Street
Washington, D.C. 20001-1512
Phone: (202) 624-5300

National League of Cities
www.nlc.org
1301 Pennsylvania Avenue, NW–Suite 550
Washington, D.C. 20004
Phone: (202) 626-3000

National State Geographic Information Council
www.nsgic.org
2105 Laurel Bush Road, Suite 200
Bel Air, MD 21015
Phone: (443) 640-1075

Urban and Regional Information Systems Association
www.urisa.org
1460 Renaissance Drive–Suite 305
Park Ridge, IL 60068
Phone: (847) 824-6300

U.S. Conference of Mayors
www.usmayors.org
1620 Eye Street, NW
Washington, D.C. 20006
Phone: (202) 293-7330

User groups

Regional user groups are excellent resources for learning more about new applications, methodologies and practices, and ideas for better managing a GIS. For a complete list of local ESRI user groups, go to *gis.esri.com/usersupport/usergroups/usergroups.cfm*.

ESRI regional user groups

CA/HI/NV/GUAM Regional User Group
www.cahinv.org
California, Hawaii, Nevada, Guam
2800 Cottage Way, MS–400
Sacramento, CA 95825–1898
Phone: (916) 978-5266

ESRI Mid-Atlantic User Group (ESRIMUG)
www.esrimug.org
District of Columbia, Maryland, Virginia, West Virginia
P.O. Box 10821
McLean, VA 22102
Phone: (703) 849-0614

Midwest ArcUser Group
igic.gis.iastate.edu/Members/bcutler/info/maug-2005
Arkansas, Illinois, Indiana, Iowa, Kansas, Kentucky, Michigan, Minnesota, Missouri, Nebraska, North Dakota, Ohio, South Dakota, Wisconsin
611 N. Walnut Grove
Bloomington, IN 47405–2208
Phone: (812) 855-5812

NEARC
www.northeastarc.org
Connecticut, Maine, Massachusetts, New Hampshire, New York, Rhode Island, Vermont
180 High Street
Wakefield, RI 02879
Phone: (401) 789-9331 x267

Northwest ESRI User Group
www.nwesriusers.org
Alaska, Idaho, Montana, Oregon, Washington
600 S Walnut
Box 25
Boise, ID 83707
Phone: (208) 287-2722

South Central Arc User Group
www.scaug.org
Louisiana, Mississippi, Oklahoma, Texas
20 North Broadway
Oklahoma City, OK 73102-8260
Phone: (405) 228-8390

Southeastern Regional User Group (SERUG)
www.serug.com
Alabama, Florida, Georgia, North Carolina, South Carolina, Tennessee
11465 Johns Creek Parkway, #460
Duluth, GA 30097
Phone: (678) 417-1883 x11

Southwest User Group (SWUG)
www.swuggis.org
Arizona, Colorado, New Mexico, Utah, Wyoming

Data sources and warehouses
Data for a local government GIS can be obtained from numerous sources, both public and commercial.

EROS Data Center
edc.usgs.gov

Federal Geographic Data Committee
www.fgdc.gov

GEO-DATA Explorer (GEODE)
geode.usgs.gov

Geography Network
www.geographynetwork.com

Geospatial One-Stop
www.geodata.gov/gos

GIS Data Depot
data.geocomm.com

MapMart
www.mapmart.com

National Atlas
www.nationalatlas.gov

National Wetlands Inventory
wetlands.fws.gov

USGS, The National Map
nationalmap.gov

Magazines, periodicals, and newsletters

Magazines, periodicals, and newsletters help keep practitioners up-to-date on the latest trends in methodology and emerging technology.

ArcNews
www.esri.com/news/arcnews

ArcUser
www.esri.com/news/arcuser

American City and County
www.americancityandcounty.com

GDT News
www.geographic.com/news/index.cfm

GIS.com
www.gis.com

GIS Lounge
gislounge.com

Government Technology
www.govtech.net

International Journal of GIS
www.tandf.co.uk/journals/titles/13658816.asp

GEOEurope
www.geoplace.com/ge

Photogrammetric Engineering & Remote Sensing
www.asprs.org/publications/pers

Professional Geographer
www.aag.org/ProGeog/intro.htm

URISA News, Journal, and Marketplace
www.urisa.org/publicat.htm

Other resources

APA National Conference GIS Implementation Seminar
www.esri.com/apa

ESRI Virtual Campus-GIS Library
campus.esri.com/library

National Center for Geographic Information and Analysis
www.ncgia.ucsb.edu

Universities
www.ucgis.org
www.esri.com/highered

ESRI publications

A partial listing of ESRI publications relevant for local government officials and managers.
- *Confronting Catastrophe: A GIS Handbook*
- *Disaster Response: GIS for Public Safety*
- *GIS and Land Records: The ArcGIS Parcel Data Model*
- *GIS for Health Organizations*
- *GIS in Public Policy: Using Geographic Information for more Effective Government*
- *Government Matters Newsletter*
- *Managing National Resources with GIS*
- *Measuring Up: The Business Case for GIS*
- *Thinking About GIS*
- *Transportation GIS*
- *Zeroing In*

ICMA publications

The ESRI-ICMA Executive Briefing Series includes free short reports (8–16 pages) detailing specific GIS applications. Available titles include
- Local Government: GIS Solutions for Community Development and Public Works
- GIS Solutions for Community Development
- GIS Solutions for Urban and Regional Planning: Designing and Mapping the Future of Your Community with GIS
- Mapping the Future of Law Enforcement
- Homeland Security: GIS for Community Safety
- Removing the Guesswork: Mapping and Managing Assets Across Local Government Operations
- GIS and Brownfields: Encouraging Redevelopment, Public Involvement, and Smart Growth

Glossary

Terms

bandwidth. Refers to the amount of data that can flow through a communications channel, unusually expressed in hertz for analog circuits and it bits per second (bps) for digital circuits. Available bandwidth is an important consideration in the ability of a local government to deliver Web-based GIS subscription services and whether users will have easy access to those services.

base data layer. Map data over which other information is placed. The base data layer serves as the foundation upon which the rest of the GIS is built.

CAD system. An automated system for the design, drafting, and display of graphical information. Short for computer-aided design, a CAD system is often used by architects and engineers to develop blueprints and schematic drawings of building and infrastructure.

contours. Lines on a map that show the different points of equal elevation, usually on land surfaces. Contours can show how steep a hill is or the slope of a river bank.

data layer. Within a GIS, a data layer represents a collection of similar types of data for a given geographic area.

enterprise GIS. An integrated, multidepartmental GIS that is composed of interoperable components. It provides broad access to geospatial data, a common infrastructure upon which to build and deploy GIS applications, and significant economies of scale.

firewall. A computer software program that provides Internet security and privacy protection for a personal computer, computer network, or network server.

Gantt chart. A work plan display that uses a combination of text and graphics to communicate the implementation schedule for a given projects. It visually shows the tasks, durations, and workflow sequences in relationship to each other, and is useful for showing the connections between different elements of a plan.

geocoding. Involves assigning x,y coordinates to tabular data such as street addresses or ZIP Codes so that they can be displayed as points on a map.

global positioning systems (GPS). A constellation of twenty-four satellites, developed by the U.S. Department of Defense, that orbit the earth at an altitude of 20,200 kilometers. These satellites transmit signals that allow a GPS receiver anywhere on earth to calculate its own location. A GPS is used where precise positioning is necessary.

hyperspectral technology. A type of remote sensing technology that acquires multispectral images in many, very narrow, contiguous spectral bands along the visible light spectrum.

Java. Akin to a universal translator, Java is a type of computer technology that enables software to run on many different kinds of systems and devices.

lidar. A remote sensing technology that uses laser to measure distances to reflective surfaces. Short for light intensity detection and ranging.

MIME file. A protocol for handling non-ASCII text in electronic mail messages. Short for multipurpose Internet mail extensions.

parcel. A tract or plot of land. The term is usually used in the context of land use or legal ownership of property.

plug in. Software programs that extend the capabilities of an Internet browser in a specific way, for example, the ability to edit data while using the browser.

primary data layer. A data layer containing fundamental data needed for the operation of a GIS.

remote sensing. Collecting and interpreting information about the environment and the surface of the earth from a distance, primarily by sensing radiation naturally emitted or reflected by the earths' surface or from the atmosphere, or by sensing signals transmitted from a satellite and reflected back to it. Examples of remote sensing methods include aerial photography, lidar, radar, and satellite imaging.

Web portal. A collection of interconnected Web sites focused on a particular issue, area, or topic.

Software programs mentioned

ArcEditor™. A complete GIS desktop system for editing and managing geographic data. The program supports single-user editing as well as a collaborative process between many editors. An extensive set of tools is included for simple data cleanup and input as well as for sophisticated design and versioning.

ArcInfo®. A complete GIS out of the box, ArcInfo provides all the functionality for creating and managing a GIS. This functionality is accessible via an easy-to-use interface that is customizable and extensible through models, scripting, and applications.

ArcGIS®. An integrated collection of GIS software products for building a complete GIS. The ArcGIS framework enables the user to deploy GIS functionality and business logic wherever it is needed—in desktops, servers (including the Web), or mobile devices. This architecture, coupled with the geodatabase, gives the user the tools to assemble intelligent geographic information systems.

ArcGIS Survey Analyst. An extension to the ArcGIS family of desktop products that allows the user to manage survey data in a geodatabase, and display survey measurements and observations on a map.

ArcSDE®. A server software product used to access massively large multiuser geographic databases stored in relational database management systems (RDBMSs). Its primary role is to act as the GIS gateway to spatial data stored in a RDBMS.

ArcView®. Considered a standard in the GIS world, the software program allows the user to easily create maps, and add new data to them. Using ArcView's visualization tools, the user can access records from existing databases and display them on maps.

References
1. Based on definitions drawn from *Dictionary of GIS Terminology.* 2001. Redlands, Calif.: ESRI Press.

Samples of legal documents

Terms and conditions for digital data request

Sample GIS Data Disclaimer

1. Limitations
Requester seeks access to the data described in the attached request. The County makes no warranty, expressed or implied, concerning the data's content, accuracy, currency or completeness, or concerning the results to be obtained from queries or use of the data. **ALL DATA IS EXPRESSLY PROVIDED "AS IS" AND "WITH ALL FAULTS".** The County makes no warranty of fitness for a particular purpose, and no representation as to the quality of any data. Users of data are responsible for ensuring the accuracy, currency, and other qualities of all products (including maps, reports, displays and analysis) produced from or in connection with County's GIS data. No employee or agent of County is authorized to waive or modify this paragraph. If a user informs others that a product is based upon County's data, the County specifically requests and directs that the user also disclose the limitations contained in this paragraph and in paragraph 4.

2. Data Interpretation
County data is developed and maintained solely for County business functions, and use or interpretation of data by the Requester or others is solely their responsibility. The County does not provide data interpretation services.

3. Spatial Accuracy
Map data can be plotted or represented at various scales other than the original source of the data. The Requester is responsible for adhering to industry standard mapping practices that specify that data used in a map or analysis, separately or in combination with other data, will be produced at the largest scale common to all datasets.

4. No County Liability
County shall not be liable to the Requester (or transferees or vendees of Requester) for damages of any kind, including lost profits, lost savings or any other incidental or consequential damages relating to the providing of the data or the use of it. The Requester shall have no remedy at law or equity against the County in case the data provided is inaccurate, incomplete, or otherwise defective in any way.

5. Requester's Warranty Against Commercial Use of Lists
[State Law reference: RCW 42.17.260(9)] prohibits the release of lists of individuals requested for commercial purposes, and Requester expressly represents that no such use of any such list will be made by Requester or its

employees, agents, transferee(s) or vendee(s). "Commercial purposes" means to facilitate any profit expecting activity.

6. Secondary Data Dissemination

Requesters may not secondarily disseminate (give County data to other entities) without prior written permission from County.

7. Project Data

Requesters are encouraged to supply their project data back to the County for use by the County.

8. Cost of Providing Digital Data

The cost of providing GIS digital data is $76.00 (seventy-six dollars) per hour plus the cost of media or transmission. The cost is the actual cost to prepare the requested data files from the County GIS database.

_____   _____
Signature of County Data User   Date Submitted

Richland County GIS
Data License Agreement

Date _____

User's Name _____
Company/Agency _____
Address _____
City _____ Zip _____
Phone _____ Fax _____
E-mail _____

PRODUCT LICENSING AGREEMENT
TERMS AND CONDITIONS

THIS LICENSING AGREEMENT is made as of the date specified on the cover hereof between Richland County (hereinafter referred to as "COUNTY") and
_____ (hereinafter referred to as the "USER").

Whereas, COUNTY is the designer and developer of the product(s) delivered under this agreement (hereinafter referred to as "DATA") with the right to license and distribute the DATA; and

Whereas, the USER will make use of the DATA in its business activity according to the following restrictions and obligations;

Whereas, the USER desires a license to use the DATA and the COUNTY desires to grant such a license to the USER for the sole purpose of permitting the USER to use the DATA in its business activity;

NOW, THEREFORE, in consideration of the premises and other good and valuable consideration, the receipt and sufficiency of which are hereby acknowledged, the parties agree to the following terms and conditions:

ARTICLE 1   PRODUCT DEFINITION

1.1   DATA includes COUNTY *digital* databases, graphic files, associated documentation, and programs which are made available for distribution.

ARTICLE 2   REPRESENTATIONS AND WARRANTIES

2.1   Limited Warranty
 (A) COUNTY shall make reasonable efforts to ensure that the DATA is delivered in a condition suitable for its proper use.
 (B) COUNTY disclaims any other warranties, express or implied, respecting this agreement or the DATA.
 (C) The DATA and ASSOCIATED MATERIALS ARE PROVIDED "AS IS", WITHOUT WARRANTY AS TO THEIR PERFORMANCE, MERCHANTABILITY, OR FITNESS FOR ANY PARTICU-LAR PURPOSE. The entire risk as to the uses, results, or performances of DATA is assumed by the USER.

2.2   The execution, delivery, and performance of this Agreement are within the USER's power and authority, and the USER has duly authorized, executed, and delivered such Agreements and has taken or will take all action necessary to carry out and give effect to the transactions contemplated by the Agreement.

ARTICLE 3   USE

3.1   Permitted Use
 (A) This license is granted for the sole purpose of permitting the USER to use the DATA in its business activity and for no other purpose whatsoever. Permitted use does include customized research and analysis. Additional permitted uses include the generation of map products and reports through the manipulation of DATA, subject to all restrictions in this agreement.
 (B) This agreement constitutes a single-user license. The USER is permitted use of the DATA, as per the conditions of this agreement, as an individual or within a single business unit or agency. The licensed use of the DATA is not governed by any intergovernmental agreements or policies.

3.2   Restrictions on Use
 (A) The USER shall not disclose, lease, sell, distribute, make, transfer, or assign the DATA or engage in any other transaction that has the effect of transferring the right of use of all or part of the DATA.
 (B) The USER shall inform COUNTY of any inaccuracies that are identified in the DATA. COUNTY will make the required changes upon appropriate verification and make corrected data available.
 (C) All USER designed materials and output (internal reports, maps, products, etc.) will bear all copyright, trademark, and other proprietary notices required by COUNTY.
 (D) USER may not publish, in the public domain, COUNTY data in any form without written approval of the County.
 (E) All USER materials will bear the date of the DATA. (Example: "Source: Richland County, insert date the DATA was most recently acquired).
 (F) All USER materials are required to be updated according to the most recent DATA available from the COUNTY.

3.3 Reserved Rights
(A) COUNTY shall retain all rights, title, and interest in the DATA, including the right to license the DATA covered by this license to other USERS.
(B) COUNTY shall retain the right to embed copyright, ownership, transactional, and licensee information in the DATA using watermarking, steganographic, or other digital techniques that do not diminish the functional capacity of the DATA.

ARTICLE 4 TERM/TERMINATION
4.1   This Agreement may be terminated by COUNTY at any time if the USER fails to comply with any of the terms of the Agreement.

ARTICLE 5 REMEDY
5.1   USER'S sole and exclusive remedy for breach of this limited warranty will be to return the DATA, which may be replaced by COUNTY at its discretion.

5.2   Any available remedy to COUNTY shall be cumulative and shall be in addition to every other remedy given under this Agreement now or hereafter existing at law or in equity or by statute. No delay or omission to exercise any right or power accruing upon any default shall impair any such right or power or shall be construed to be a waiver thereof; nor shall any single or partial exercise of any right hereunder preclude any other or further exercise thereof or the exercise of any other right. In order to entitle the COUNTY to exercise any remedy available to them in this Article, it shall not be necessary to give notice other than such notice as may be required by law.

ARTICLE 6 RELEASE AND INDEMNIFICATION
6.1   COUNTY shall not be liable for any activity involving the DATA with respect to the following:
(A) Lost profits, lost savings, or any other consequential damages.
(B) The fitness of the DATA for a particular purpose.
(C) The installation of DATA, its use or the results obtained.

6.2   COUNTY shall not be liable for indirect, special, incidental, compensatory, or consequential damages or third-party claims resulting from the use of DATA, even if they have been advised of the possibility of such potential loss or damage.

6.3   RELEASE AND INDEMNIFICATION. The USER, *to the extent allowed by state law*, hereby releases the COUNTY and the State and their respective officers, directors, members, employees, attorneys, and agents, (hereinafter collectively referred to as "Indemnified Parties") from, and agrees that such Indemnified Parties shall not be liable for, and agrees to indemnify and hold harmless the Indemnified Parties against any or all liability or loss, cost, or expense, including without limitation, attorney's fees, fines, penalties, and civil judgments, resulting from or arising out of or in connection with or pertaining to any loss or damage resulting from the use of the DATA.

ARTICLE 7 MISCELLANEOUS
7.1   **Invalidity.** To the extent that any provision of this Agreement is determined to be in contradiction of, or in conflict with the Code, any State law, or any regulation, the Code, State law or regulation shall control.

7.2 Entire Agreement. This LICENSE contains the entire agreement of the parties hereto with respect to the matters covered hereby, and no other agreement, statement, or promise made by any party hereto, which is not contained herein, shall be binding or valid.

7.3 Governing Laws. This Agreement is made under and shall be construed in according with the laws and regulations of the State of South Carolina. By executing this Agreement, the USER agrees to submit to the jurisdiction of the COUNTY and the Courts of South Carolina for all matters arising hereunder. In the event of a dispute, the COUNTY shall have standing to represent the State of South Carolina.

7.4 Amendment. This Agreement may be changed or amended only by written agreement of the parties.

Witness the hands and seals of the parties this day and date first above written:

Richland County, South Carolina
Information Technology/GIS Department

USER

_____
Signature

_____
Signature

_____
Title

_____
Title

_____
Date

_____
Date

Terms and conditions for GIS regional subscription services

AGREEMENT FOR ONLINE ACCESS TO COUNTY INFORMATION SYSTEMS

The terms of this Agreement will remain in full force and effect for a five (5) year period ending on _____, 20 ___, subject to thirty (30) days written notice of termination by either party to the other.

The parties, in consideration of the terms and conditions described below, agree as follows:

SCOPE OF SERVICE

1. The **County** agrees to provide the services described in Exhibit A (referred to as Service) according to the terms of this agreement. **Requestor** agrees to provide access to and use of the Service and all other resources necessary to use the Service under this agreement.

FEE FOR SERVICE

2. **Requestor** agrees to pay for the services in accordance with the rates or charges set forth in Exhibit A(s). The **County** will notify the **Requestor** 30 days in advance, in writing, of annual service rate changes. The **County** will bill the **Requestor** quarterly with terms of net cash, payable within thirty (30) days after the statement date. **Requestor** shall pay all applicable taxes related to use of the Service by **Requestor**. Non-payment for Services shall result in the termination of the Services.

CONDITIONS OF USE

3. **Requestor** represents and agrees that the **County** information and systems will not be used for commercial purposes contrary to the requirements of **RCW 42.17.260(9)** and **WAC 390-13-010**.

4. **Requestor** agrees not to use the Service, nor any of its elements or related facilities or capabilities, to conduct any business or activity, or solicit the performance of any activity that is prohibited by or would violate any applicable law, rule, regulation or legal obligation.

5. The parties agree that should **Requestor** use this Service in a manner contrary to the terms of this Agreement, **Requestor** will be ineligible to receive any similar service in the future and **Requestor** will be subject to all applicable civil and criminal penalties. Misuse or damage of service components or County data could result in billable charges for actual damages.

6. The **Requestor**, its officers and employees, will:
   a. Maintain the confidentiality of **County** information.
   b. Comply with **Pierce County Data Dissemination Disclaimer** (Appendix C) and refrain from releasing or providing Pierce County data to other entities (secondary data dissemination). Since this County Policy is based on RCW(s) and ordinances, changes are made annually and will be provided at the same time as the annual service rates (as stated in Section 2).
   c. Maintain the proprietary nature of Pierce County software, data, and systems used by the **Requestor** under the terms of this Agreement.
   These conditions shall be met except upon the prior written consent of the steward County department and the Pierce County Prosecuting Attorney, or an order entered by a court after having acquired jurisdiction over the **County**.

7. **Requestor** will immediately give to the **County** notice of any judicial proceeding seeking disclosure of **County** information by contacting the Pierce County Prosecuting Attorney's Office.

8. **Requestor** agrees not to transmit, upload, post, or otherwise publish on or over the Service, and not seek on or over the Service, any software, file, information, communication or other content
   a. that violates or infringes upon the rights of any other;
   b. that, under the circumstances and in **County's** good faith judgment, is, or is likely to be perceived by an intended recipient or target as, defamatory, deceptive, misleading, abusive, profane, offensive or inappropriate;
   c. that constitutes a threat to, harassment of, or stalking of another;
   d. that adversely affects the performance or availability of the Service or County resources;
   e. that contains any virus, worm, harmful component, or corrupted data; or
   f. that, without the approval of the **County**, contains any advertising, promotion, or solicitation of goods or services for commercial purposes.
   g. that allows unauthorized access to **County** data and systems.

9. Subject to the terms of this Agreement, the **County** grants to **Requestor** and authorized users a personal, nonexclusive, nonassignable and nontransferable license to use and display the software (referred to as Software) provided by or on behalf of **County** for purposes of accessing the Service on any machine(s) of which **Requestor** is the primary user or that **Requestor** is authorized for use. Unauthorized copying of the Software, including software that has been modified, merged or included with the Software, or the associated written materials is prohibited. **Requestor** may not sublicense, assign, or transfer this license or the Software except as permitted by **County**.

LIABILITY

10. The information supplied by the **County** pursuant to this Agreement is provided on an "as-is basis" and "with all faults" and **Requestor** will have no remedy at law or equity against the **County** in the event information provided to the **Requestor** is inaccurate, incomplete, or otherwise defective in any way.

11. The **Requestor** agrees to hold the **County**, its appointed and elective officers and employees, harmless from any and all claims, liability, fines, judgements, settlements and penalties, including attorney fees and costs, made by any person as a result of making such information available to **Requestor** for **Requestor's** use.

SYSTEM OPERATIONS

12. The **County** retains the right to modify current systems at its discretion. The **County** will make no systems modifications on **Requestor's** behalf unless specifically detailed in Exhibit A. The **Requestor** is responsible for ascertaining the impact of changes on their business.

13. **Requestor** agrees that each and every person given the right to access **County** systems will use a unique user name assigned by Pierce County Information Services staff. Each user will sign the most current system and security agreement(s) (Exhibit B) and return to Pierce County Information Services with written request for security access.

14. **Requestor** understands that priority is assigned to regular **County** work which may require a reasonable delay in responding to **Requestor's** requirements from time to time. The **County** shall not be held liable for service interruptions.

15. **Requestor** is to provide and maintain all required service components necessary to connect to **County** services in the manner authorized by the **County**.

16. **Requestor** is to ensure that all equipment and software used to access the Pierce County systems defined in Exhibit A, will be compatible with existing **County** configurations.

17. **Requestor** agrees to keep the **County** informed of any network connectivity between them and other organizations.

18. **Requestor** understands and agrees that online access will be available only between the hours of 8:00 AM and 5:00 PM Pacific Time, Monday through Friday, exclusive of legal holidays observed by the **County**. Limited online access may be available outside of these hours. The **County** shall not be held liable if the system/network is off-line and not accessible.

CONTACTS

19. The **County** will provide a list of contacts to administer the Services provided under this agreement.

20. **Requestor** will provide the names of at least two (2) of their employees who will be the primary contacts with Pierce County staff. Requests for new users, user modifications, or user assistance will come from these contacts. A method of verification will be provided to these employees to use when identifying themselves to Pierce County.

21. **Requestor** is to contact the **County** and request deletion of a staff's user name within 24 hours following notice of termination of their employment with the **Requestor**.

SPECIAL PROVISIONS

22. Network Security

In an attempt to prevent the loss of information/data and to minimize the costly effects of network/system security attacks or system maintenance and network downtime, the County reserves the right to terminate, immediately and without notice, Requestor connection(s) to County resources if it appears that Requestor's continued connection to County systems appears to be harmful (i.e., for example, virus, worm, or network security attacks) to either County or Requestor. Connection will not be reinstated until County determines that such threat no longer exists. Reasonable care and timeliness will be taken to re-establish connection to the Requestor. By accessing the County system, Requestor acknowledges the right and discretion of County to terminate Requestor's connection(s) in the event of a network security threat and agrees that County will not be liable to Requestor for interruption of business or in any other fashion in regard to any such termination or failure to terminate. If County staff must provide assistance to Requestor to ensure Requestor's systems are free from harmful threats, charges will be assessed as described in Exhibit A attached

ATTACHMENT 1

Definitions
1. Service Service or Services is defined as this contract between the Requestor and the County to provide the work products described in Exhibit A, Scope of Work.

2. Annual Service Rates. The fees and charges for the Service(s) from the County that will be reviewed and adjusted yearly as described in Exhibit A, Scope of Services.

3. Commercial Purposes. The commercial use of the County data is prohibited per RCW 42.17.260(9). This statue says that the County systems and data may not be used to produce lists of names or contact individuals for commercial use or purpose.

4. Steward Departments. One, or in some cases multiple, County departments are designated as the steward of each particular named computer system and its corresponding set of information media (data files, databases, screens, views, reports, menus, and query access). As such, steward departments have the authority to determine data access methods, the dissemination mechanism, and secondary data dissemination rules (primary data dissemination rules are specified in a separate County policy statement) for any request to access such systems and information media. In order to execute this authority, steward departments are responsible for the maintenance of security, accuracy, and integrity of the computer systems and information media.

EXHIBIT A
SCOPE OF SERVICES
This PAGE describes the scope of the subscriptions services, deliverables, and support.

EXHIBIT B
PIERCE COUNTY COMPUTER NETWORK AND INFORMATION SECURITY ACCESS AGREEMENT for Employees, Contractors, Volunteers, and External Agency Employees.

Access to the Pierce County Network has been provided to you so you may complete specific activities related to your job duties or contractor agreement. Any use beyond what is agreed upon and described in your duties/contract is not allowed. Security will be in place to limit your activities on the network. By signing this agreement, you state that you will not attempt to access information or services not meant to be available to you on the Pierce County network as described in your assigned duties.

You also agree to safeguard any passwords provided to you to access Pierce County systems. You must configure your access to the Pierce County network so that a password must be typed in each time you access the system(s). You cannot share this password with any one else. Log out of Pierce County systems whenever you cease working on the system or whenever you are away from your computer.

You are responsible for any damage caused by actions you take on the Pierce County network that are outside of those described in your duties/contract.

You are to use the utmost discretion in preserving the confidential nature of any information you are authorized to access. Information is to be obtained for authorized purposes ONLY. Obtaining any information for personal use is prohibited; this includes looking up information in any of the computer databases for personal use. As an employee or contractor you may not observe, obtain, nor ask another person to obtain confidential information for personal reasons. You shall not disclose information of a confidential nature. Releasing information may be in violation of the laws of the State of Washington, for example a violation of the provisions of the Criminal History Privacy Act (RCW 10.97) shall constitute a misdemeanor and may result in criminal prosecution. When in doubt, be discreet, and talk with your Pierce County supervisor/contact. It is better to err on the side of caution than on the side of carelessness.

I have read and understand the above policy regarding computer network access and confidential information and have received copy of same.

Agency/Employer _____

Date: _____ Employee/Contractor Signature:_____

Terms and conditions for use of local government software products

**Richland County GIS
Data License Agreement**

Date _____

Any notices required hereunder from Richland County or its representatives to USER shall be effective if made to the below-listed employee or representative, or his/her successor of USER as set forth below:

Date _____

User's Name _____
Company/Agency _____
Address _____
City, State _____ Zip _____
Phone _____ Fax _____
E-mail _____

PRODUCT LICENSE AGREEMENT TERMS AND CONDITIONS

THIS LICENSE AGREEMENT is made as of the date specified on the cover hereof between Richland County (hereinafter referred to as "COUNTY") and __xxxx (hereinafter referred to as the "USER").

Whereas, COUNTY is the designer and developer of the commercially valuable product(s) delivered under this agreement (hereinafter referred to as "SOFTWARE") with the right to license and distribute the SOFTWARE; and Whereas, the USER will make use of the SOFTWARE in its business activity according to the following restrictions and obligations; Whereas, the USER desires a license to use the SOFTWARE and the COUNTY desires to grant such a license to the USER for the sole purpose of permitting the USER to use the SOFTWARE in its business activity; NOW, THEREFORE, in consideration of the premises and other good and valuable consideration, the receipt and sufficiency of which are hereby acknowledged, the parties agree to the following terms and conditions:

ARTICLE 1 Representations, Warranties, and Covenants.

1.1   Each party to this Agreement represents and warrants that:
  (a) it has full legal right, power, and authority to enter into this Agreement and to perform and consummate all other transactions contemplated by this Agreement;
  (b) it has duly authorized the execution, delivery, and performance of its obligations under this Agreement and the taking of any and all actions as may be required on the part of each party to perform and consummate the transactions contemplated by this Agreement;
  (c) this Agreement constitutes a legal, valid, and binding obligation of each party, enforceable in accordance with its terms; and
  (d) there is no action, suit, proceeding, inquiry, or investigation at law or in equity before or by any court, public board, or body, pending or, to the best of the knowledge of each party, threatened against either party, nor to the best of the knowledge of each party is there any basis therefore, which in any manner questions the powers of either party to this Agreement, or the validity of any proceedings taken by either party or its governing body in connection with this Agreement or wherein any unfavorable decision, ruling, or finding could materially adversely affect the transactions contemplated by this Agreement or which, in any way, would adversely affect the validity or enforcement of this Agreement (or of any other instrument required or contemplated for use in consummating the transactions contemplated thereby and hereby).

ARTICLE 2 Product Definitions.

2.1   SOFTWARE includes computer language, code, syntax, interfaces, graphics, and associated documentation developed by the COUNTY that are made available for distribution.

2.2   "Derivative Works" are works that, in any manner, expand, enhance, or diminish the functionality, capabilities, interface, or documentation of any portion of the SOFTWARE.

ARTICLE 3 License Grant.

3.1   Subject to the terms and conditions herein, COUNTY grants to USER a limited, nontransferable, nonexclusive, single site license to use the SOFTWARE for which this license is purchased, and to develop Derivative Works, as defined herein. Under the terms of this license Agreement, USER is a single organizational unit constituting the local government known as [NAME of LOCAL GOVERNMENT], [STATE], authorized to use the SOFTWARE and to develop Derivative Works internally at a single site.

3.2   USER must notify COUNTY of Derivative Works. USER must make all Derivative Works available to COUNTY for a licensing fee not to exceed the fee paid to COUNTY for SOFTWARE covered under this license.

ARTICLE 4 Limited Warranty and Disclaimer of All Other Warranties.

4.1   COUNTY shall make reasonable efforts to ensure that the SOFTWARE is delivered in a condition suitable for its proper use.

4.2   COUNTY disclaims any other warranties, express or implied, respecting this agreement or the SOFT-WARE. The SOFTWARE and ASSOCIATED MATERIALS ARE PROVIDED "AS IS," WITHOUT WARRANTY AS TO THEIR PERFORMANCE, MERCHANTABILITY, OR FITNESS FOR ANY PARTICULAR PURPOSE. The entire risk as to the uses, results, or performances of SOFTWARE is assumed by the USER.

ARTICLE 5   Use.

5.1   Permitted Use. This license is granted for the sole purpose of permitting the USER to use the SOFTWARE in its business activity and for no other purpose whatsoever.

5.2   Restrictions on Use
  (A)   The USER shall not disclose, lease, sell, distribute, make, transfer, or assign the SOFTWARE or engage in any other transaction that has the effect of transferring the right of use of all or part of the SOFTWARE.
  (B)   The USER shall inform COUNTY of any inaccuracies, bugs, or errors which are identified in the SOFTWARE.
  (C)   USER installed SOFTWARE will include comment lines indicating the rights of the COUNTY as the developer of SOFTWARE. Maintained SOFTWARE documentation will also indicate the rights of the COUNTY as the developer of the SOFTWARE.

5.3   Reserved Rights—COUNTY shall retain all rights, title, and interest in the SOFTWARE, including the right to license the SOFTWARE covered by this license to other USERS. Title and ownership to the SOFT-WARE delivered hereunder and any copies made by USER in whole or in part are and shall at all times remain in COUNTY. USER acknowledges COUNTY'S claim that the SOFTWARE contains valuable proprietary information and trade secrets and that unauthorized dissemination of the SOFTWARE (including, without limitation, disassembly, decompiling, or reverse engineering) could cause irreparable harm to COUNTY and therefore USER agrees not to make the SOFTWARE available to any person unless USER has taken appropriate action with any such person permitted access to the SOFTWARE so as to satisfy USER'S obligations hereunder. USER shall not make copies of the SOFTWARE except a single back-up copy of magnetically recorded SOFTWARE that is delivered on tape, magnetic disk, or other volatile media to protect against SOFTWARE destruction. USER will reproduce and include all copyright and other proprietary notices on any back-ups made in accordance with COUNTY'S and its suppliers' instructions.

ARTICLE 6   Term/Termination.

6.1   This Agreement shall commence once signed by an authorized representative of each party and may be terminated by COUNTY at any time if the USER fails to comply with any of the terms of the Agreement.

ARTICLE 7   Remedies.

7.1   USER'S sole and exclusive remedy for COUNTY'S breach of any term or condition of this Agreement will be to return the SOFTWARE, which may be replaced by COUNTY in its sole discretion.

7.2   Any available remedy to COUNTY shall be cumulative and shall be in addition to every other remedy given under this Agreement now or hereafter existing at law or in equity or by statute. No delay or omission to exercise any right or power accruing upon any default shall impair any such right or power or shall be construed to be a waiver thereof; nor shall any single or partial exercise of any right hereunder preclude any other or further exercise thereof or the exercise of any other right. In order to entitle the COUNTY to exercise any remedy available to it in this Article, it shall not be necessary to give notice other than such notice as may be required by law.

ARTICLE 8   Release and Indemnification.

8.1   COUNTY shall not be liable for any activity involving the SOFTWARE or USER's or USER's agents or assigns, whether permitted hereunder or not, including, but not limited to the following:

(A) lost profits, lost savings or any other consequential damages.

(B) the fitness of the SOFTWARE for a particular purpose.

(C) the installation of SOFTWARE, its use, or the results obtained.

8.2   COUNTY shall not be liable for indirect, special, incidental, compensatory, or consequential damages or third-party claims resulting from the use of SOFTWARE, even if they have been advised of the possibility of such potential loss or damage.

8.3   The USER hereby releases the COUNTY and the State and their respective officers, directors, members, employees, attorneys, and agents, (hereinafter collectively referred to as "Indemnified Parties") from, and agrees that such Indemnified Parties shall not be liable for, and agrees to indemnify and hold harmless the Indemnified Parties against any or all liability or loss, cost, or expense, including without limitation, attorney's fees, fines, penalties, and civil judgments, resulting from or arising out of or in connection with or pertaining to any loss or damage resulting from the use of the SOFTWARE.

ARTICLE 9   Miscellaneous.

9.1   Invalidity. To the extent that any provision of this Agreement is determined to be in contradiction of, or in conflict with the Code, any State law, or any regulation, the Code, State law or regulation shall control.

9.2   Entire Agreement. This Agreement contains the entire agreement of the parties hereto with respect to the matters covered hereby, and no other agreement, statement, or promise made by any party hereto, which is not contained herein, shall be binding or valid. No agreement hereafter made between the parties shall be binding on either party unless reduced to writing and signed by an authorized officer or agent of the party sought to be bound thereby. The parties agree that should any provision, clause, term, paragraph, or phrase of this agreement be rendered void or ineffective by the order of any court, then the remaining terms of the agreement will remain in full force and effect.

9.3   Governing Laws. This Agreement is made under and shall be construed in accordance with the laws and regulations of the State of South Carolina. By executing this Agreement, the USER agrees to submit to the jurisdiction of the COUNTY and the Courts of South Carolina for all matters arising hereunder.

9.4   Publicity. No publicity releases (including news releases and advertising) relating to this Agreement and the provision of SOFTWARE hereunder (other than a brief announcement upon contract execution) shall be issued by USER without the prior written approval of COUNTY. Any inquiry that USER may receive from news media concerning this Agreement will be immediately referred to COUNTY for approval prior to response.

9.5   Nonappropriations. This Agreement and all contracts entered into by COUNTY resulting form this Agreement shall be subject to cancellation without damages due from or further obligation of COUNTY when funds are not appropriated or otherwise made available to support continuation of performance in any fiscal period or appropriated year.

USER AND COUNTY ACKNOWLEDGE THAT THEY HAVE READ THIS AGREEMENT, UNDERSTAND IT, AND AGREE TO BE BOUND BY ITS TERMS. NO MODIFICATIONS SHALL BE EFFECTIVE UNLESS IN WRITING AND SIGNED BY BOTH PARTIES.

IN WITNESS WHEREOF WE THE UNDERSIGNED have this _____ day of _____, 2002, set our hand and seal hereon.

_____   WITNESSES:

_____   _____
By:
Its: _____

RICHLAND COUNTY   WITNESSES:

_____   _____
By:
Its: _____

Index

See glossary for a comprehensive list of terms used in this book.

Advanced Spatial Analysis: The CASA Book of GIS *1-58948-073-2*
ArcGIS and the Digital City: A Hands-on Approach for Local Government *1-58948-074-0*
ArcView GIS Means Business *1-879102-51-X*
A System for Survival: GIS and Sustainable Development *1-58948-052-X*
Beyond Maps: GIS and Decision Making in Local Government *1-879102-79-X*
Cartographica Extraordinaire: The Historical Map Transformed *1-58948-044-9*
Cartographies of Disease: Maps, Mapping, and Medicine *1-58948-120-8*
Children Map the World: Selections from the Barbara Petchenik Children's World Map Competition *1-58948-125-9*
Community Geography: GIS in Action *1-58948-023-6*
Community Geography: GIS in Action Teacher's Guide *1-58948-051-1*
Confronting Catastrophe: A GIS Handbook *1-58948-040-6*
Connecting Our World: GIS Web Services *1-58948-075-9*
Conservation Geography: Case Studies in GIS, Computer Mapping, and Activism *1-58948-024-4*
Designing Better Maps: A Guide for GIS Users *1-58948-089-9*
Designing Geodatabases: Case Studies in GIS Data Modeling *1-58948-021-X*
Disaster Response: GIS for Public Safety *1-879102-88-9*
Enterprise GIS for Energy Companies *1-879102-48-X*
Extending ArcView GIS (version 3.x edition) *1-879102-05-6*
Fun with GPS *1-58948-087-2*
Getting to Know ArcGIS Desktop, Second Edition Updated for ArcGIS 9 *1-58948-083-X*
Getting to Know ArcObjects: Programming ArcGIS with VBA *1-58948-018-X*
Getting to Know ArcView GIS (version 3.x edition) *1-879102-46-3*
GIS and Land Records: The ArcGIS Parcel Data Model *1-58948 077-5*
GIS for Everyone, Third Edition *1-58948-056 2*
GIS for Health Organizations *1-879102-65-X*
GIS for Landscape Architects *1-879102-64-1*
GIS for the Urban Environment *1-58948-082-1*
GIS for Water Management in Europe *1-58948-076-7*
GIS in Public Policy: Using Geographic Information for More Effective Government *1-879102-66-8*
GIS in Schools *1-879102-85-4*
GIS in Telecommunications *1-879102-86-2*
GIS Means Business, Volume II *1-58948-033-3*
GIS Tutorial: Workbook for ArcView 9 *1-58948-127-5*
GIS, Spatial Analysis, and Modeling *1-58948-130-5*
GIS Worlds: Creating Spatial Data Infrastructures *1-58948-122-4*
Hydrologic and Hydraulic Modeling Support with Geographic Information Systems *1 879102-80-3*
Integrating GIS and the Global Positioning System *1-879102-81-1*
Making Community Connections: The Orton Family Foundation Community Mapping Program *1-58948-071-6*
Managing Natural Resources with GIS *1-879102-53-6*
Mapping Census 2000: The Geography of U.S. Diversity *1-58948-014-7*
Mapping Our World: GIS Lessons for Educators, ArcView GIS 3.x Edition *1-58948-022-8*
Mapping Our World: GIS Lessons for Educators, ArcGIS Desktop Edition *1-58948-121-6*
Mapping the Future of America's National Parks: Stewardship through Geographic Information Systems *1-58948-080-5*
Mapping the News: Case Studies in GIS and Journalism *1-58948-072-4*
Marine Geography: GIS for the Oceans and Seas *1-58948-045-7*
Measuring Up: The Business Case for GIS *1-58948-088-0*
Modeling Our World: The ESRI Guide to Geodatabase Design *1-879102-62-5*
Past Time, Past Place: GIS for History *1-58948-032-5*

Continued on next page

When ordering, please mention book title and ISBN (number that follows each title)

Books from ESRI Press (continued)

Forthcoming titles from ESRI Press

Ask for ESRI Press titles at your local bookstore or order by calling 1-800-447-9778. You can also shop online at www.esri.com/esripress. Outside the United States, contact your local ESRI distributor.

ESRI Press titles are distributed to the trade by the following:

In North America, South America, Asia, and Australia:
Independent Publishers Group (IPG)
Telephone (United States): 1-800-888-4741 • Telephone (international): 312-337-0747
E-mail: frontdesk@ipgbook.com

In the United Kingdom, Europe, and the Middle East:
Transatlantic Publishers Group Ltd.
Telephone: 44 20 8849 8013 • Fax: 44 20 8849 5556 • E-mail: transatlantic.publishers@regusnet.com

ESRI Press • 380 New York Street • Redlands, California 92373-8100 • www.esri.com/esripress